Professionals
Stepping Up

"From time to time, in the course of human events, someone develops a great idea which proves to be transformative. With the publication of *Stepping Up: A Companion and Guide for Family Caregivers*, Cenetta J. Lee and Gloria F. Carr, Ph.D., RN, have put in one place for the first time every valuable insight and critical information piece necessary to perform the priceless service of caring for a loved one in need of aid and assistance."
— Prince C. Chambliss, Jr., Attorney, Author, Adjunct Law Professor, Cecil C. Humphreys School of Law, The University of Memphis, Memphis, Tennessee

"*Stepping Up* will serve as a guide to others going through similar situations. … As a professional caregiver, it helps me to understand the feelings of a family going through this with someone they love and respect."
— Anna Bradford, RN, DSHA, Director of Nurses, Kirby Pines Retirement Community, The Manor, Memphis, Tennessee

"From professional and now personal experience, my wish for each of us facing profound family changes in our society is to have this marvelous tool to help guide our way. *Stepping Up* will be a lifeline for everyone-daughter or son, child or parent."
— Marcia West, BSN, HCA, Director of Professional Services, Retired Interim Healthcare, Richmond, Virginia

"During my eleven years as an Orthopedic Surgeon, I have observed the recovery and comfort of my patients improves after surgery when there is a devoted family advocate. Many of the topics discussed in *Stepping Up* will help relatives understand their importance to ailing loved ones. *Stepping Up* is a valuable resource for all families—young and more mature when a loved one experiences a life-changing situation."
— Jack W. Bowling Jr., Orthopedic Surgeon, Bowling Orthopedics, Wilmington, North Carolina

"As a Social Worker for a hospital I encounter many situations in which family members have not communicated long-term plans with their aging loved one. It is very important to discuss things early to avoid stressful situations down the road. It's often difficult to discuss things such as Nursing Home placement and End of Life Care—but to honor someone's wishes, communication is a must."
— Ava McDonald, BSW, Director of Social Services, Dosher Memorial Hospital, Southport, North Carolina

"Finally, a book based on personal experience for those looking for help during a difficult time in life. I love this book, and highly recommend *Stepping Up* to caregivers, medical professionals and clinicians who work with those experiencing transformations in health."
— Norman Mitchell, M. Div. Bereavement/ Grief Counselor,
Crossroads Hospice, Memphis, Tennessee

"*Stepping Up* by Cenetta J. Lee and Gloria F. Carr provides a valuable resource for our nation's near thirty percent of the population: family caregivers, and for those who provide services to family caregivers. It serves as a companion to family caregivers as it guides family caregivers with tangible, practical, and useful information and necessary steps to provide care for loved ones while maintaining balance and promoting well-being of caregivers."
— Lin Zhan, Ph.D., RN, FAAN, Professor and Dean of The Loewenberg School of Nursing,
The University of Memphis, Memphis, Tennessee

"At a time when our society is placing increased emphasis and importance on the benefits of multigenerational families, and the need to strengthen internal family relationships, Cenetta Lee and Gloria Carr have provided us with a comprehensive look at successful caregiving within a family setting."
—Ernest A. DiMattia Jr., President, The Ferguson Library, Stamford, Connecticut

"In this life we are usually presented a whole plethora of "how to" options for things that may or may not be significant in our living. What Lee and Carr do in *Stepping Up* is give us a guide that is as practical as it is readable; it is as timely as it is honest, and for the readers who choose to read this book before being in this situation, this work will help prepare us a little bit better for something one can never totally prepare for."
—Dr. Walter L. Parrish III, General Secretary Progressive National Baptist Convention
Incorporated, Washington, D.C.

"Today's seniors and their children expect much more of their retirement than the generation before. Yet few are truly prepared for the paths that they will have to go down to age successfully. *Stepping Up* provides a map to assist both parent and child (caregiver) with the necessary tools to travel down this path."
—Michael Escamilla, Director, Kirby Pines Retirement Community, Memphis, Tennessee

"I found *Stepping Up* to be an incredible resource, leaving no area not explored. The recommendations and associated tools are not only valuable but essential to those embarking on this journey. Thank you for writing this."
—Mary Jane Stillwagon, RN, BSN, Administrative Director for Performance Improvement
Medical/Surgical/Critical Care Services, Duke University Hospital, Durham,
North Carolina

Stepping Up

A Companion and Guide for Family Caregivers

Cenetta J. Lee and Gloria F. Carr, Ph.D., RN

PHRONESIS
PRESS

Southport, North Carolina

Stepping Up
A Companion and Guide for Family Caregivers

PHRONESIS
PRESS

Published by
Phronesis Press
PO Box 10967
Southport, North Carolina 28461

ISBN: 978-0-9839622-0-5

Library of Congress Control Number: 2011942573

Printed in the United States of America

Book and cover design
Jeanie James, Shorebird Media

Cover and chapter photos: Fotolia.com and Shutterstock.com

First trade printing 2012

10 9 8 7 6 5 4 3 2 1

Disclaimer: *Stepping Up* provides advice to help family caregivers through their difficult task. But this book is not a substitute for professional medical, legal, or financial advice. The Authors have presented only an overview of the medical, legal, and financial issues that you need to address. Every situation is different. If you are a family caregiver or you are working with a family caregiver, you are encouraged to seek the advice of medical, legal and financial professionals.

The legal documents presented in this book are samples only. They are not intended as forms for actual use in your situation. The applicable laws differ from state to state, jurisdiction to jurisdiction, circumstance to circumstance. Use these samples for your general information only. In no way are these sample documents substitutes for appropriate legal advice or for documents properly prepared by a duly qualified attorney.

Dedication

To the glory of God.

To our beloved families.

To loyal family caregivers.

Acknowledgments

So many individuals have played a part in my journey and thus in this labor of love—writing this book. My gratitude goes first to God for the gift of life. Then to my parents Harold and Ida Jamison for instilling in my sisters Carole J. Parrish, Alva J. Crawford and me the love of family and Godly values.

My appreciation goes to many relatives who provided help and support during this project. First, my husband of 53 years, Charles Lee; my children—Ceneta Lee-Williams and Charles Augustus Lee, who were the second pair of hands to teach me from life's learning laboratory how to love and be loved; my son–in–law Johnny Williams and my daughter-in-law Patricia Edwards Lee; my grandchildren, Chantal Reneé Williams, Caitlin Ida Lee, and Sophia Margaret Lee.

I feel sincere gratitude for several who provided medical and other professional advice during this journey: Drs. Alvin H. Crawford, James O. Patterson III, Melvinie Seymore, Bradley Somer, James Boone, Elbert Hines III, Theresa Holmes, RN; the nurses and staff at Baptist East Hospital, West Clinic, The Med, Parkway Health and Rehabilitation Center, and Kirby Pines Retirement Community, all in Memphis, Tennessee; my legal advisors, Judge Carolyn Brackett, Prince Chambliss, Laurice Smith, and Preston Wilson; Jesse Turner, Jr., CPA; my many practitioners who kept me as balanced as possible most of the time; Kelle Eli, who taught me to stay where God is in my heart through all the big and little bumps on my timeline. Without these people I would not be here to share my journey. Thank you for showing up and doing your part with genuineness and integrity.

Additional recognitions are due the many hands that so willingly aided in the writing of this book. I thank my husband for being able to live with me during the last phase of completing this book. He spent many hours creating several forms in the appendix and in being a sounding board throughout this endeavor. Gratitude goes to Dr. Gloria Carr,

Assistant Professor of Nursing at University of Memphis for joining me in writing this book. Her professional knowledge and experience is exceptionally valuable to the coverage of caregiving. We started working together on this project as strangers and finished as friends for life. A special thanks goes to Maryann Canu for sharing her ideas and experiences from a practicing and teaching nurse perspective.

I extend my heartfelt expressions of gratitude to the following individuals who allowed me to share with you their personal experiences—Reverend Melvin Lee, my brother-in-law; and my friends, Sue Fegan and Dr. John O'Brien. I am indebted to Dr. Mark A. Stebnicki for writing a compassionate Foreword. To those who read this manuscript and offered advice during the writing of this book: Aleta Boyd, Janet Chaney, June Fleming, Bradley Harris, Ann Hazelton, Murray McCord, Dr. Melvinie Seymore, Marcia West, Ceneta Lee-Williams and Patricia Edwards Lee, I sincerely appreciate your friendship and help.

To those many cherished family members and close friends who, directly or indirectly, knowingly or unknowingly made a contribution to the writing of this book—Carole and Walter L. Parrish II, Alva Crawford, Dell A. Crowder, Sandra and Jesse Parks, Patricia Hoy, Clara McAdams, Bryce McAdams Jr., Alvin and Charlotte Crawford, Carole Crawford, and others too numerous to mention—my heartfelt thanks for their encouraging me through their words, prayers, and positive thoughts.

I owe a great deal of gratitude to Sheryl Stebbins for her professional editorial experience, her friendship led me to Jennifer McCord, the person who put life into my manuscript. Through my editorial consultant, Jennifer McCord, *Stepping Up* gained a new momentum because of her encouragement and professional editing of the final manuscript—thank you, Jennifer McCord. I could not have done it without you.

Additional thanks goes to the hands-on caregivers for my aunts and my mother. Their everyday care and love helped set examples for me as I learned to be patient and grateful.

Table of Contents

Foreword

STEPPING UP IS an exceptionally timely, unique, and comprehensive body of work that was created to help family members recognize changes in their loved ones' medical, emotional, cognitive, and mental status. This text indeed steps up to the challenge that confronts many baby-boomers and caregivers today that are oftentimes forced to provide the sole care for family members who can no longer manage his or her health, finances, and activities of daily living.

This material is extraordinary because it offers much more than a review of the literature and discussion of the issues. The reader will find that the material in *Stepping Up* is practical and particularly functional for caregivers. It offers a very close, up-front, personal, and experiential account from its authors of issues relating to the mental, emotional, physical, and spiritual exhaustion that occurs when working at intense levels in the caregiver role with their loved ones. One of the most valuable lessons offered in this unique body of work suggests that one of the hardest things for untrained caregivers to do, is to know what, how, and when to intervene on behalf of a relative or loved one. This work goes beyond advice or consultation and offers readers sample legal and healthcare documents that are essential for optimal care, protection, and advocacy for older Americans. Thus, *Stepping Up* offers much more than a discussion of caregiver grief, loss, and burnout. It is a primary source material that educates, informs, and provides a rich knowledge base for future planning for the compassionate care of one's family members.

As I reviewed *Stepping Up* I was amazed at how comprehensive this body of work is. For more than 25 years, I have worked in the fields of rehabilitation, mental health, guardianship and advocacy, and counselor education. I am an active psychotherapist, counselor educator, and psychosocial researcher that have had to rely on multiple resources throughout my career. As most practitioners can tell you there are only a few selected resources that are typically found on their office bookshelf; ones that are more valuable resource and frequently used. This best depicts the material assembled in *Stepping Up* because it is extensive, reader-friendly, and exceptionally functional. The authors provide special care in organizing the material using a practical approach so as to not overwhelm the reader with too much technical information.

The resource list and body of knowledge in *Stepping Up* is very personal and compassionate. However, this work is much more than just a collection of personal and anecdotal stories. It is complemented by the integration of valid research from the medical and healthcare fields such as New England Journal of Medicine, psychosocial care material such as Elisabeth Kübler-Ross classical works on death and dying, nationally-known professional associations such as the American Heart Association, as well as many more citations which suggests to me that exceptional care was given by its authors to provide the reader with quality and accurate information.

I found the chapters in *Stepping Up* to be well written, organized in a clear and concise manner, and presented in a well-informed and balanced way. This will be a valuable resource not only for caregivers but also for professionals that work in programs and services for older adults. *Stepping Up* could also be used as a primary source for training others for the care, compassion, protection, and advocacy of older Americans. Overall, *Stepping Up* is a wellstone of information written by authors who have much compassion and knowledge to share with others.

— Mark A. Stebnicki, Ph.D., LPC, CRC, CCM
   Professor and Director of Graduate Program in Rehabilitation Counseling
   College of Allied Health Sciences
   East Carolina University, Greenville, NC

Introduction

According to the National Family Caregivers Association, the need for family caregivers will increase in the coming years. The number of people over 65 is expected to increase at a 2.3 percent rate while the number of family members available to care for them will only increase at a 0.8 percent rate. The aging population will increase and the younger population will decrease. In addition, the typical family caregiver is a 46-year-old woman caring for her widowed mother who does not live with her. Thirty percent of family caregivers caring for seniors are themselves aged 65 or over, and another 15 percent are between the ages of 45 and 54. Apparently, future caregivers will be younger; caring for more than one loved one and possibly including more males.

This reference guide was written for future generations of caregivers—Boomers aged 45 to 64, Generation X aged 30 to 46 and Generation Y aged 16 to 29 to prepare for the inevitable role of caring for their parents, grandparents and other loved ones. I was a family caregiver for three loved ones over a period of nine years, and Dr. Gloria Carr acquired her geriatric knowledge from many years of professional experience as a nurse and Assistant Professor of Nursing at The University of Memphis. This book is our effort to help future caregivers recognize when it is time to ask questions or even intervene on a loved one's behalf when deteriorating health has begun.

We wrote *Stepping Up: A Companion and Guide for Family Caregivers* to achieve two important tasks. First, this book was created to help you to recognize signs of a loved one's change in medical, emotional and cognitive status. And, secondly, it will help determine what is needed as you care for your aging loved one as a family caregiver.

The following factors are discussed in depth:

- signs and symptoms of declining health

- caring for loved ones at home and its related tasks

- managing care outside the home

- locating and supervising care from a far distance

- medical services issues

- diseases and conditions of the elderly—strokes, cancer and dementia

- services available toward the end-of-life; tasks after death

- essential legal documents

- and there are tips, books, on-line and agency resources

Also, *Stepping Up* includes opportunities for family members to journal their responses to questions and document their experiences as a family caregiver.

Assisting you to be prepared to care for your parents or other loved ones after a life-changing experience is our mission. Knowing how to do needed tasks, in addition, to learning through our experiences will help your time as a caregiver to be less stressful and challenging.

Chapter One

Becoming a Caregiver

I believe every human mind feels pleasure in doing good to another.
— Thomas Jefferson

IN RECENT YEARS, family members from the younger generation have assumed the role of family caregivers. According to the Family Caregiver Alliance, "Caregivers can be found across the age span, the majority of caregivers are middle-aged (35-64 years old)."[1] In some cases, it is often multiple older generation family members who are being cared for because the population is living longer. So, you may have a mother and a grandfather to care for at the same time or you may need to help an older family member care for an even older relative. "Many caregivers of older people are themselves elderly. Of those caring for someone aged 65 or over, the average age of the caregiver is 63 years with one third of these caregivers in poor health."[2] Therefore it is important to become informed and prepared in case you may have to assume the caregiver role for your family in the future.

1 Family Caregiver Alliance. Selected Caregiver Statistics, 2010.
2 Ibid.

For example, I moved back to my hometown. My mother was the family healthcare advocate and had Power of Attorney for her oldest sister. Because Mother had failing health, she was unable to visit my aunt to regularly check on her. I agreed to assist Mother. Two family members—Mother and I—began sharing the family healthcare advocacy and Power of Attorney responsibility. Mother knew the history of my aunt's health and business affairs and I was able to execute what needed to be done and made regular visits.

The unpredictability of when a family member will need you to care for them is a key factor in making preparations in advance. For instance, in the cases of Catherine, Joyce, Larry, and Sandra outlined below, it never occurred to them that one life-changing situation would suddenly make family care-giving a reality.

An Elderly Aunt Becomes Ill

AFTER 25 YEARS of living coast-to-coast, Catherine, age 50, and her husband moved back to the city of their birth. They returned because her husband took a job at the local university. Catherine and her husband had two children, aged 22 and 24 years old. Their 24-year-old daughter has an 18-month-old daughter. She and her family live in another city. She is their first grandchild and they are enjoying grandparenthood.

In the city where Catherine and her husband were born, many family members still live there, including Catherine's mother, two aunts and a cousin. On her husband's side of the family, his father, three brothers, and a cousin also live in their hometown. When they returned home, they had lived away from both of their families for some time. Visits were not as frequent as expected but each family felt supported. Their parents were visited at least once a week by local relatives and they talked with them regularly.

One day after completing her errands, Catherine received a frantic telephone from her cousin saying her beloved Aunt Catherine was taken to the hospital. "I'll be right there," Catherine said. She didn't live far from her aunt so Catherine drove to her aunt's house. She picked up her cousin to accompany her to the local hospital. They sat for hours in the Emergency Room waiting area waiting to hear the diagnosis from the doctor. They saw her aunt as the hospital staff took her for a procedure. The staff allowed them to say something to her. They kissed her on the forehead and said, "We'll be right here waiting for you. We love you."

Catherine and her aunt share the same name, as Catherine was born on her aunt's birthday. Growing up, they would visit Aunt Catherine maybe twice a month to check on her. She didn't have any children and lived alone.

As the cousins sat waiting for hours, they realized that they were now wondering what the next stage of life will bring for their aunt and themselves. Should they have talked to their aunt about her aging and her health?

Taking Over a Family Held Business

JOYCE, AGE 63, lives with her husband of 35 years in Indianapolis, Indiana. She has a 28-year-old son from a previous marriage. Joyce is an administrator in the Indianapolis Public Schools system. She enjoys her job but misses the direct contact with students and parents.

Life as empty nesters is perfect for Joyce and her husband. They travel nationally and internationally when their budget and schedules allow. She enjoys antique shopping on the weekends, playing tennis, and attending the opera.

Joyce grew up in an entrepreneurial family. Her parents own and operate a 90-year-old floral business their grandfather founded when he was a young man. He developed a passion for the floral business while working as a teenager in a florist shop assisting with designs and deliveries. The family florist shop continues to serve Indianapolis area residents.

When Joyce's father died five years ago, her mother ran the business profitably with the help of her loyal staff. Recently, Joyce's mother mentioned that the business' revenue was fluctuating each quarter. Joyce and her husband didn't grow concerned because it often happens with businesses. However, her mother became ill and went to the hospital for a few weeks where she was diagnosed with advanced ovarian cancer. They were asked to manage the business. While reviewing the financial records, it became apparent that the monthly expenses exceeded the monthly revenue and the business was losing money.

Joyce and her husband concluded that now was not the time to talk about this with her mother because it might hamper her recovery. They now found themselves in charge of her mother's healthcare as well as determining the fate of the family's floral business. As Joyce began to manage her mother's health and business finances, she told her husband she wished they had talked about business and health concerns with her before her illness.

Single Parent and Elder Relative

A SINGLE PARENT, Larry, age 40, and his son live in Pasadena, California. The weather is pleasant throughout the year with no snow in the winter or heat and humidity in the summer. Residents only have to carry an umbrella during the rainy season.

Larry works very hard to provide his son with a loving home. Three years ago, he experienced a tough divorce. The court awarded Larry custody of his son and eventually he became both father and mother to him. At times, he wondered how other single parents do it, but he loves his son. He doesn't have the help of his parents because they are deceased. However, Larry's favorite aunt lives close by and helps to raise his son, which he is very grateful for.

After getting his son off to his junior high school, Larry commutes to work for 45 minutes. As he was listening to his favorite music and the morning news, he got a call on his cellphone from his beloved aunt. In a faint voice she told him that she had just fallen down the stairs and that she couldn't get up. Thank goodness he encouraged her to keep her portable telephone with her at all times because she was able to call him for help. He asked her if she had called her neighbors but she told him that they weren't home.

Since he did not know how serious the fall was or how his aunt was doing, he called 911 and gave them all of the pertinent information. They requested her telephone number so that they could keep her on the phone until the Emergency Medical Services (EMS) or Larry arrived.

Larry arrived before EMS and he found his aunt lying at the bottom of the stairs on the floor on her side. He gently held her hand and assured her that EMS would be there soon. EMS arrived, took her vital signs, and stabilized her for the ride to the hospital.

They arrived at the hospital and although the doctors suspected a broken hip, they performed the necessary tests to confirm their assumption. Larry's aunt would need hip replacement surgery, immediately. The decision is made to do the surgery. As Larry thinks about her recovery and her medical care, he realizes that they will have to do some planning quickly to accommodate this change in their lives.

Unexpected Health Events

SANDRA, AGE 29, was born, raised, and works in Boston, Massachusetts. She maintains constant contact with her family who live close by. Her mother is widowed and her daughter sees her throughout the week and has talked with her daily since her father's death.

Sandra is married to the kind of man she dreamed of when she was growing up. They met in college and married a few years after graduating. Sandra's husband, Sam, is a loving husband and a great father to their two young children—18 months and 4 years old. They have responsible careers and they are determined to provide a comfortable lifestyle for their family.

One Monday, Sandra went to work and prepared for an early morning planning meeting of her department. As the meeting progressed, she noticed the receptionist hurriedly walking toward the conference room. She opened the door quietly, walked to Sandra and whispered to her that she had an emergency call. Sandra went to her office to take the urgent call and the person explained that they were in the Boston Medical Center Emergency Room and that her mother had just arrived. They needed her there immediately with her mother's medical history so they could start treating her.

A coworker offered to drive her to the hospital to help Sandra with this unexpected news. When they arrive at the hospital emergency room, they introduce themselves to staff and were taken to her mother. The nurse told Sandra they were trying to stabilize her so they could perform the necessary tests on her.

The friend suggested that Sandra call her husband and siblings. Sandra wonders what happened, she sounded okay. But as she thinks back on the previous days and weeks, she recalls having noticed a few changes in her behavior—she seemed occupied, less talkative, and complained about a headache. Now she realizes that she should have paid more attention to the warning signals.

> *Could have … should have … would have …* are among the regrets you are guaranteed to experience in your life.

> *I should have gotten to know a loved one better … paid attention to their complaints … kept records of family medical history … talked to them about their wishes when a serious illness or death occur … observed them more thoroughly … helped them make life plans … shared my personal preferences with them …*

These and other choices will have to be made by loved ones at a highly emotional time if these discussions haven't happened before a life changing situation occurs.

THESE BRIEF DESCRIPTIONS of family situations are just a few of the many examples of how quickly and unexpectedly you may become a family caregiver for an elderly relative. This responsibility may become yours willingly or unwillingly. Life-changing situations for an elderly family member may happen quickly or slowly but it will eventually happen to all of us. The situations presented here may or may not be similar to what will happen to you; however, it is wise to prepare yourself in advance to reduce the future impact on your life. The stress occurs when you have to continue to live your life while determining what to do to help your elderly family member. We wrote this book to help you become more prepared and efficient in eventually helping care for your parent, sibling, aunt, uncle, or cousin. The blueprint for being a family caregiver has yet to be written because families, situations, and individuals are so different. But, the basic tasks covered in our book will need to be considered as you move into the role of caregiver for your elderly family member.

Journal
Becoming a Caregiver

- **Which family member(s) will need my help soon?**

_____

_____

_____

- **What are the signs that indicate they need help?**

_____

_____

_____

_____

- **What ways can I help?**

_____

_____

_____

_____

- *Additional notes:*

Chapter Two

Recognizing Symptoms of Declining Health

I ask not for a lighter burden, but for broader shoulders.
—Jewish Proverb

SYMPTOMS OF DECLINING health are often related to altered body functioning of the sick body part. For those providing care to a loved one, general symptoms are listed below. This list is not all-inclusive but rather offers general symptoms of declining health so that family caregivers may recognize when their loved one's health changes. As always, it is best for them to see their family doctor when you discover any of these symptoms, but awareness of these symptoms may also influence prompt involvement of health care providers.

Declining Health

SOME OF THE SYMPTOMS of declining health include:

Appearance

» Poor hygiene

» Disheveled appearance

» Worsening health problems

» Self-neglect

» Unsteadiness

» Weight loss

Nutrition

» Loss in appetite and weight

» Weakness and low energy

» Inability to take medications independently

Communication

» Confused

» Repeating themselves during conversation

» Lack of socialization/decreased desire to communicate

» Forgetfulness

» Altered concentration and impaired judgment

» Sleeping more frequently during the day

Behavior

» Erratic behavior (e.g., driving into the wrong driveway of their home)

» Depressed/lack of interest in what's going on in life and environment

» Complaining about the same physical problem

» Chronic insomnia/restlessness

» Being reclusive

» Mood changes

▶ ***Professional Case Example:*** *A family caregiver (a daughter) noticed that her mother started having the inability to hold her urine until she was in the bathroom. After several weeks, the mother was taken for a routine doctor's visit. At the visit, the daughter informed the doctor of the situation. Tests were completed and revealed that the mother had a urinary tract infection.*

Outcome: Antibiotics were prescribed and the mother did not have further incontinence after completing the antibiotics. Therefore, any change in the patient requires further examination by a healthcare provider.

Note: If an ailing family member displays unusual mental behavior, ask their nurse and doctor to perform the test for a urinary tract infection (UTI). You may have to be persistent but do so because one urinary tract infection symptom for an older adult is often mistaken for a mental disorder. You do not want your family member diagnosed and admitted to a mental facility when the real problem is a urinary tract infection instead.

THIS BOOK IS designed for those who are caring for a family member who can no longer manage his or her health and daily living. Whether your family member is elderly or incapacitated by an accident or illness, you are now that person's advocate and spokesperson.

One of the hardest things for an untrained caregiver is to know when to act on behalf of a relative and what to do to help them. Because every situation is different, there isn't a set pattern of actions that you'll need to take. We encourage you, however, to use this book as a guide.

As you care for your family member, you may notice that his or her health isn't improving and recovery is slow. These symptoms don't necessarily indicate a decline in health—they could be side effects of medication. But don't try to guess what the problem is. It is always prudent to share your concerns with your family member's doctor. The doctor will want your loved one to schedule an appointment. He or she will determine what is causing the changes and what can be done to address them.

Dealing with Your New Feelings

YOU WILL NOTICE that you are feeling sad as you take on these responsibilities. The idea of losing a family member is haunting and you fear it occurring before it happens. It is when you recognize that your elderly family member is showing signs of physical and cognitive decline that the thought of death really comes to mind. This is a normal process that you are going through and it will continue to happen throughout the remainder of this journey.

Experts have offered many symptoms for this feeling of anticipatory grief. According to the American Hospice Foundation, "The worst symptoms of all—anxiety and dread—illustrate this point." The Foundation cites *Death and Identity*, a book by Robert Fulton, Ph.D. and Robert Bendiksen, Ph.D. They explain that "You expect your loved one to die, but exactly when it will take place is not known."[1] This creates suspense and you live wondering if it will be today or tomorrow or months or years from now. Once you think it will happen, you dread it actually occurring.

What seems to help is talking about it with a close friend, support service, or to journal about what you are feeling as soon as you experience those thoughts or feelings. Unfortunately, these symptoms vary in intensity, happen repeatedly, or sometimes may occur together. When you don't acknowledge what is happening, you can't do anything about it.

---

1 American Hospice Foundation. *www.americanhospice.org.*

Journal

Recognizing Symptoms of Declining Health

- ***Have you as caregiver or family member recognized changes in any of your elder family members? List family member and associated changes.***

_____

_____

_____

_____

_____

_____

_____

_____

_____

_____

_____

_____

Journal

Dealing with Your New Feelings

- **Today, I had these feelings:**

_____

_____

_____

_____

- **I did these things to control these feelings:**

_____

_____

_____

_____

- **The following actions were successful for me:**

_____

_____

_____

_____

Chapter Three

Talking with Elder Family Members

Speech is the mirror of the soul; as a man speaks, so is he.
— Publilius Syrus

WHEN YOU ARE talking with aging parents or elderly family members, sharing your thoughts will help to establish mutual respect and trust. Once trust is established getting to a common goal is easier. Effective communication is based upon mutual understanding and finding a solution that works for all parties, not winning or being right. Communication is the key element to all successful relationships.

Communicating with an aging parent is a little different because of the parent-child relationship. The common goal of loving each other may often be lost in translation. The parent may not recognize your concern about their welfare because you will always be their child not an adult who is capable of making very important life-changing decisions. And, we may just see our parents as "old." Change isn't easy for either side, but as the saying goes, "The one thing in life you can be sure of is change." With our parents, we have to patiently accept their changes and still express our loving concern.

In addition to communicating effectively with parents, you must also be able to talk with aunts, uncles, siblings, or cousins when they need your help. The techniques for communicating with other relatives are the same as talking with your parents. In some ways, it may be easier because your parents will always think of you as a child.

If the family members of your relatives are unable to step up to help their loved one during this time of crisis, the ailing family member will be appreciative and grateful for your help. The ailing loved one will help you with this process as much as they are physically and cognitively able. They will be happy to talk about themselves and their life. You just have to be a good listener. If you identify a relative showing defiance and becoming confrontational, you may have to ask a neutral person they respect for help in encouraging cooperation and understanding.

Helping other relatives besides your parents will provide you the opportunity to become reacquainted with them. Remember to refrain from speaking negatively of the persons who refused to take on this responsibility. It takes a special type of person to share their lives with others to help them deal with an illness or life-changing situation. Keep in mind that others may not have the stamina to deal with this type of medical distress. We all have our strengths and weaknesses, and if this is your strength, think of it as a blessing from God that you were given the gift to help others in their time of need.

IF YOU HAVE established and maintained a loving relationship with regular communication and visits, discussing the noticed decline in an elder's health will be easier. Visits are extremely important because you can't see by telephone how the elderly are walking or if they are keeping themselves well groomed. If you aren't communicating and visiting with them, you will need to start as soon as you can. When the time comes to talk about possible health changes, they may listen to you when you suggest going to their doctor if you have already established a loving and supportive relationship with them.

Depending upon how an elder family member is aging, the responsibility for acknowledging the potential medical change in their health will be up to them. Acknowledgment may not be immediate but keep asking about it and eventually they will say you were right about the change in their health, which may lead to a doctor's appointment. Be prayerful for their awakening to the need for getting professional medical advice. This is a major challenge for all of us, so remain patient and lovingly concerned.

THESE ARE SOME techniques to use when communicating with elderly parents or family members:

- Be aware and sensitive to how you respond when talking to an aging or cognitively-challenged person. Sometimes, they can't find the words to say what they want to say or it takes them longer to find them.
- Know that the older person usually understands and is aware of far more than they can say in words.
- Create a comfortable environment to have conversations.
- Smile and touch them as you talk.
- Make a guess at what their response might be and see if they shake their heads in the affirmative that may say, "That's right."
- Use a normal speaking voice and talk slowly if you are a fast talker.
- Try changing the pitch of your voice (low or high) if you think there's a hearing problem not addressed.
- Display positive body language—eye contact, good posture, and a smile.
- Restate your message concisely and straightforward.
- Be patient.
- Set boundaries when conflict arises while scheduling medical appointments by saying "no" to a request that is either unreasonable or untimely. When possible, ask if the appointment can be scheduled for another time.
- Treat them with respect.
- Comfort and use a soothing tone, take them for a walk, or change the scenery when you notice anxiety, confusion, or fear arising.
- Listen attentively with participation, openness, and receptivity.
- Make a positive statement when they are complaining. If you continue to do this, it will get their attention and they will realize they are complaining and stop.
- Think before you respond and practice silence when you are upset or angry.
- Reminisce with them—"Dad, I remember when Auntie …"
- If cognitive changes are significant, don't ask pointed questions like "Who am I?" Say, "Mom. It's your daughter …"
- If there is difficulty speaking, connect in another way by massaging their hands and arms gently, combing their hair, polishing their nails, or reading to them. This makes them feel appreciated and lets them know you love them.
- Praise! Praise! Praise! Show appreciation for your parents. Let them know you realize they tried to do the best they could and acknowledge the desire to pass these good characteristics on to your children.

Journal
Talking with Elder Family Members

- **What family members do I need to talk with about family, health, and life transition issues?**

_____

_____

_____

_____

- **What questions do I want to discuss with them?**

_____

_____

_____

_____

_____

_____

_____

_____

- ***What memories can I share with them?***

_____

_____

_____

_____

_____

_____

- ***How can I involve other family members?***

_____

_____

_____

_____

_____

_____

_____

- *Additional notes:*

_____

_____

_____

_____

_____

_____

_____

_____

_____

_____

_____

_____

_____

_____

Chapter Four

Caring for Your Loved Ones

The simple act of caring is heroic.
—Edward Albert

YOUR NEXT STEP will be gathering your loved one's legal documents. Once you find them, read them thoroughly so you know what documents are available, what still need to be executed, and who is responsible for handling various aspects of your relative's life. The following three personal experiences point out the importance of having this information readily available.

> ❧ *Personal Experience: The need for legal documents first became apparent when I had to assist my mother in caring for her oldest sister. Mother held the Power of Attorney and primary responsibility for her health care. Because my mother didn't drive, frequent visits to observe what was happening*

became impossible. After a year of observing the situation, I felt increasingly concerned. Eventually, it became apparent that Mother needed help in overseeing my aunt's care and in performing the responsibilities that are assigned with the Power of Attorney. Mother and I began to execute the legal documents needed to allow me to share in this oversight process—dealing with caregivers and making medical and financial decisions.

*❧ **Personal Experience:** My 88-year-old aunt was assaulted in her home. The perpetrator left her wounded and she was alone and bleeding for almost twelve hours. Finally, she was discovered, an ambulance was called and she was rushed to the hospital.*

The hospital doctors worked on her to determine the extent of the assault. She remained in the hospital for three weeks, rehabilitating and getting various tests performed. Her extended hospital stay demanded that action be taken to manage her business because there was no full-time person on staff to take over for her.

A respected friend recommended a lawyer. My friend made the initial contact, and I followed up by telephone. After explaining the situation to him, he drafted a Durable Power of Attorney and a Durable Power of Attorney for Healthcare and Living Will.

*❧ **Personal Experience:** In my mother's case, all legal documents were established. She had a Power of Attorney that included healthcare proxy authority. A Living Will was created eight years prior to being needed. She also had a Last Will and Testament. If this is needed, I encourage you to start earlier with this document because it takes some time for loved ones to make their decisions about their personal belongings before a final legal document can be written and signed.*

IF YOU NEED the basic information quickly, chances are that you'll find some of the information in the person's wallet or purse. For example, you may find:

- Driver's license
- Bank cards
- Insurance cards
- Bank account numbers

- Debit cards and credit cards
- Prescriptions
- Safe deposit box numbers and codes
- Sometimes names and contact information of doctors, lawyers, insurance professionals, and the like
- Business cards of professionals who may have been working with your loved one

ANOTHER LIKELY PLACE to find this information might be in the loved one's home or in a safe deposit box, or they may have provided it to an immediate family member or friend. Cellphones and personal digital assistants (PDAs) may also contain valuable contact information.

Gather all insurance policies such as health insurance, long-term care insurance, and life insurance to determine their health coverage, value, and which policies are immediately relevant. Carefully review the terms and conditions and fine print of these policies. This is the beginning of another eye-opening experience—if your name is not on the policy, the insurance company will not discuss anything with you. Before you can obtain this information, you must have the first essential legal document, which is a Durable Power of Attorney or Power of Attorney. *(See Sample Legal Documents: Durable Power of Attorney in Appendix C.)*

Assuming that no legal documents have been executed and your loved one is in an alert state of consciousness, have your loved one privately discuss with a lawyer their wishes and sign a document declaring who will represent them in the event they are unable to make their own decisions. If the person is unconscious or in a coma or does not have a spouse, *you'll need to petition the courts to appoint a guardian. In either case, someone is needed to make decisions for them in the event that their medical or psychological condition worsens.*

By the way, a home safe is a very secure place to store these important documents. However, if an unconscious loved one is the only one with the combination, a safe is of no use to anyone. Please give someone in your family the combination to your safe so that this will not happen to you.

THE SECOND STEP you need to take in preparation for your caregiving responsibility is to become thoroughly familiar with your loved one's financial situation. This is a critical step because qualification for financial assistance from many outside agencies, including the federal government, is based on need. Make a list of all assets—cash on hand, checking, savings and investment accounts, insurance policies, real estate holdings, and collectibles such as art, antiques, stamp collections, coin collections, and the like. With regard to collectibles, obtain a written appraisal from a reputable and knowledgeable person because the value of these items can have a significant impact on your loved one's total asset base and may affect their ability to qualify for financial assistance.

- **Calculate debts:** Outstanding bills, mortgages, and loans. Other expenses may become apparent as you review your loved one's checkbook or find invoices and account statements. Next, determine your loved one's income—Social Security, pensions, accounts receivable, and investment dividends. *(See sample forms in Chapter Six: Your Loved One's Personal Information.)*

- **Social Security:** If your loved one is receiving their monthly Social Security payments by check from the United States Government Social Security Administration (SSA) instead of by direct deposit, there is a critical step that you must take if you are designated as the person to handle their financial matters. You must apply for "representative payee" status with the Social Security Administration. You should be able to find this information on their website.

    *❧ **Personal Experience:** When I assumed the responsibility of my aunt after her hospitalization, it was difficult to make decisions for her personally and medically. Because she owned a business, it was a complicated situation. Durable Power of Attorney was needed in this situation. The Social Security Administration (SSA) required me to complete a form to become her representative payee. This responsibility allowed me to receive her monthly Social Security payment with my name and her name on the check.*

> **Note:** You must use the government's form—not a substitute. Accompanying this form you will need a completed signed copy of the Physician's/Medical Officer's Statement of Patient's Capability to Manage Benefits, which you can obtain from the Social Security Administration.

YOU MUST SUBMIT your loved one's **Power of Attorney and Declaration of Representative—Form 2848** to the Social Security Administration for authorization to receive their monthly payment from the SSA.

The government will mail the check as scheduled, with the loved one's name and your name printed on the check. Just remember you can't cash or sign for deposit without your name also as a payee on the front of the checks.

The SSA has established this form of responsibility so a relative, friend, or an interested party can serve as the "representative payee" of the person being cared for. The SSA investigates the caregiver and determines whether the person is fit to be paid the loved one's benefits to use on that person's behalf. Once appointed, you will receive a booklet from the SSA, *A Guide for Representative Payees,* which will clearly define your responsibilities in this role.

Tips: Social Security Administration visit
- Determine what is needed beforehand.
- Call ahead to ask about what you will need to have with you.
- Avoid going on the first of the month.
- Take picture identification and your Social Security card.
- Go when you aren't in a rush.
- Take a book or magazine to read.
- Cell phone use is prohibited.
- Answer questions thoroughly.
- If your request isn't granted immediately, ask, "How long will it take?"
- Keep a log of your visit and purpose.

ONCE YOU HAVE GATHERED the financial information, you can calculate your loved one's cash flow and their net worth. When this information is combined with the health care and medical benefits offered in your loved one's long-term healthcare policy, you can have a better understanding on how caregiving costs can be paid. If the amount needed for their care is more than your loved one's income, you will need to find sources to fill the financial gap.

    Personal Experience: In determining my aunt's finances, I discovered she qualified to apply for financial assistance and receive Medicaid. Her spending didn't exceed her income while she was home, but the cost of the rehabilitation center that she was admitted to cost more than her income and assets. Once she was in the facility, I had to provide information to qualify her again every year. I had to make certain her resources never exceeded a certain amount. The exact amount may be obtained from the state eligibility representative who interviews you.

Three options for health care assistance are:

- **Medicare**
- **Medigap**
- **Medicaid**

- **Medicare:** Medicare is a federal government insurance program for people who are age sixty-five years or older and for certain disabled people. To find out whether you qualify, go to your local Social Security office or call their hotline. If you are helping your loved one to qualify, take them with you, because you cannot inquire about a person unless they are present. Again, to represent your loved one, you must apply for representative payee status or Social Security Administration Power of Attorney. Call the Social Security Administration or search the website to find out what you need to bring.

- **Medigap:** This is a private supplemental insurance program that covers the medical bills Medicare does not pay. If your loved one has a secondary health insurance, this type of help may not be needed. Medigap will protect your loved one from ongoing medical expenses. It can be an excellent idea for the loved one who does not qualify for Medicaid but could use help. These are private insurance companies, so be sure only to inquire and pay for what your loved one needs, and be careful to read the fine print.

- **Medicaid:** A joint federal and state government medical assistance program for people with low incomes, elderly people with Medicaid coverage also qualify for Medicare. The rules for both vary so you may need to employ the services of a lawyer to get you through these rules. A few of the costs covered by Medicaid include:

  - » Physician services
  - » Laboratory and x-ray services
  - » Medical transportation
  - » Prescription drugs
  - » Inpatient and outpatient hospital services
  - » Rehabilitation and physical therapy

For a complete list of all services covered by Medicaid, contact Medicare or your State's Insurance Program at your Regional Department of Human Services (DHS). Medicare will tell you the name and contact number for your state program.

ADDITIONAL ASSISTANCE in finding financial support for you or your loved one may be obtained from the counseling services offered by your employer through their Employee Assistance Program (EAP). This assistance may eliminate the need for you to do the initial research on sources for additional resources. Ask your human resource department about their programs.

Journal
Caring for Your Loved Ones

- ***Which legal documents do I have?***

_____

_____

_____

- ***Which legal documents do I need?***

_____

_____

_____

- ***Who can recommend an attorney?***

_____

_____

- ***What information do I have regarding loved one's personal finances?***

_____

_____

_____

- **What information do I need regarding loved one's personal finances?**

_____

_____

_____

_____

_____

_____

_____

- **What information do I have regarding health, life, and other insurance policies?**

_____

_____

_____

_____

_____

_____

- ***What ideas or resources are available for obtaining additional financial support?*** *Include contact names, phone numbers/e-mail, and/or address.*

_____

_____

_____

_____

_____

_____

_____

_____

_____

_____

_____

_____

_____

_____

Chapter Five

General Legal Matters

Have peace of mind by expressing your loved one's wishes.
— Author Unknown

AS WE DISCUSSED previously, to assume your role as family caregiver, you'll need these legal documents:

- ***Durable Power of Attorney or a Power of Attorney***
- ***Durable Power of Attorney for Health Care***
- ***Living Will***

An attorney can provide you with all three notarized documents at one time. The attorney may ask you detailed questions in order to recommend the appropriate Power of Attorney for your situation. Since lawyers can be expensive, you should be as prepared as possible for lawyer's interview to minimize the time spent on educating you on the basics. Referrals from friends and others you respect can lead you to the most appropriate attorney. You will need to determine how complex the issues are for which you need a lawyer. If it's simply for the routine Power of Attorney documents, almost any lawyer would be able to help you with them. However, if your needs extend to issues with their care facilities or insurance companies, or if you anticipate any family disagreements with actions being taken, you may need to seek a lawyer with expertise in elder law.

The importance of having the essential legal documents is discussed in this section. The primary caregiver will continually need the Durable Power of Attorney or Power of Attorney and Living Will throughout the loved one's care. Upon the death of your loved one, your authority ceases and responsibility moves to the executor/executrix of their estate.

Below is a brief description of these essential documents:

Durable Power of Attorney

THIS DOCUMENT GIVES a person the power to act on another person's behalf when they become incapable of handling financial or health affairs themselves. The Durable Power of Attorney is thought of as a document primarily for the elderly. However, younger people may also wish to have one created and executed. There are times when one does not get warnings of major life-changing situations. The Durable Power of Attorney (DPOA) is different from a regular Power of Attorney. A Durable Power of Attorney stays in effect even if the people granting it become mentally incapable of acting on their own behalf. This is a very essential document that will be used over and over again. Please make certain you have multiple notarized copies. Ask your attorney whether it needs to be filed with the county clerk of the residing municipality. I suggest having ten original notarized copies. *(See Sample Legal Documents: Durable Power of Attorney in Appendix C.)*

Durable Power of Attorney for Health Care

THIS DOCUMENT GRANTS authority to the named person to make health care decisions in the event a person is unable to make them for themselves. Your loved one must be mentally competent to execute this document. Remember that only one person can be designated. However, an alternate can be identified. Healthcare POAs can be very detailed and can include items you might not have ever considered, so make sure you engage an appropriately qualified attorney who considers your individual situation thoroughly. *(See Sample Legal Documents:– Durable Power of Attorney for Health Care in Appendix C.)*

Living Will

THIS DOCUMENT INDICATES one's desires in receiving treatment in the event of a catastrophic illness. In most cases, the Living Will is required when an elderly individual is admitted to a hospital or healthcare facility. A Living Will must be very specific with regard to the type of medical treatment a person wishes to have or does not wish to have as the case may be. It covers the use of artificial life support mechanisms and other medical solutions for prolonging life. Resuscitation is an intricate issue. Review with the doctor what the different options are, and discuss with the hospital their resuscitation protocol. This is the set of procedural guidelines that an institution such as a hospital, clinic, or medical treatment service uses to determine whether or not to revive a person and return them to consciousness. This very question is the most emotional and thought-provoking subject to discuss with anyone. It is extremely difficult to think about the possibility of dying. It could take several casual discussions before a person will determine what their final wishes will be. One approach to ease into talking with a reluctant person is to discuss a situation that another person has experienced. Making the discussion less personal in this way may help the person participate more fully. However, if you feel comfortable with their openness, ask how they would want to handle this if the situation should arise. *(See Sample Legal Documents: Living Will in Appendix C.)*

Although the Last Will and Testament is not required for health care purposes, it is suggested for a loved one who has valuables or memorable possessions to insure that they are assigned according to their wishes.

Last Will and Testament

A LAST WILL AND TESTAMENT is recommended for anyone having any assets. It should be filed with the county clerk of the respective city once it is completed. ***Keep the original in a safe place: A lost original can cause a probate attorney to do extra work and thus incur more cost to the estate.*** A copy of a Will may be admissible in probate if you can explain to the court's satisfaction what happened to the original. The attorney will communicate with other family members to see if they contest the copy. In the event that the Will is lost, having to write to each immediate relative will take time and money as lawyers do charge for all time spent in obtaining and then executing a Will

THIS DOCUMENT SPELLS OUT to whom the loved one wants various assets given upon their death. Following the wishes of the person is less complicated with a Will. If your loved one passes away intestate—that is, they die without having a valid Will—the process of settling the estate will take more time and money. If the Will is contested, there will be additional cost to the estate and to those contesting, creating an invariable delay in the settlement of the estate.

IF YOU HAVE access to the Internet, visit our website at *www.eclecticcaring.com* for examples of legal websites where you can get additional information. You can then determine for yourself what course of action will prove best for your specific journey with your loved one or friend. Attached are samples of these documents. *(See Sample Legal Documents: Last Will and Testament in Appendix C.)* You can see formats for documents on many websites, so browse the Internet diligently.

> ✑ ***Personal Experience:*** *Each time Mother or my aunts went to the hospital these documents were requested. They were also required before I could learn of their condition in the many times they were admitted to the hospital. This happened whether I was in town or out of town. Because of the Health Insurance Portability and Accountability Act (HIPAA) of 1996, you must have this information on file. One of the major purposes of this rule was to protect an individual's health information.*

Journal

General Legal Matters:

- ***What questions were generated from my review of the sample legal documents?***

_____

_____

_____

_____

_____

_____

_____

_____

_____

_____

_____

_____

_____

_____

- *Additional Notes:*

Chapter Six

Your Loved One's Personal Information

The invariable mark of wisdom is to see the miraculous in the common.
— Ralph Waldo Emerson

YOUR LOVED ONE'S personal information should be accessible and current. Throughout his or her care, you will frequently need this information, including the following:

- Full name, address, phone and fax numbers
- E-mail address
- Social Security Number
- Medicare number
- Life insurance policy, company name, and policy number
- Medical insurance policies, guidelines, and policy numbers
- Legal documents like Durable Power of Attorney, Living Will, etc.

- Medical, professional, and business contacts, landlord, address, and phone number
- Bank account information
- Church name, address, and pastor
- Preferred hospital and phone numbers

Records and Document Management

Regularly update your loved one's personal information. Keep original copies of legal documents in a secure, fireproof location. You may occasionally need to produce an original copy of the legal Durable Power of Attorney or Power of Attorney, so make sure you have at least five notarized originals.

You will also need records of your loved one's bank, investment, and retirement accounts. You may locate other financial documents in your loved one's business correspondence. Keep these documents in a separate secure and convenient place.

Important contact information for your loved one

- **Family:**
  Advocate name: _____
  Home phone: _____ Cell phone: _____
  Other: _____
- **Caregiver:**
  Name: _____
  Office phone:_____ Cell phone: _____
  Schedule (days/hours): _____
- **Local Medical Facility:**
  Days and time open _____
  Phone: _____
- **Residence's Front Desk :**
  Information or emergency: _____
  Days and time open: _____
  Phone: _____
- **Doctors:**
  Dr. _____
  (Nurse's name _____) Office phone:_____
  Dr. _____
  (Nurse's name   ) Office phone: _____

Medical and Personal Contacts Form

Medical Information:
Name
Doctor
Nurse (at doctor's office)
Doctor's Office Information:
Name
Address
Phone number(s)
Pharmacy Information:
Company
Address
Phone number
Fax number
Caregiver Information:
Name
Position (e.g., CNA or RN)
Address
Phone number(s)
Fax number

Insurance Information

Insurance provider
Type of insurance
Policy # Group #
Company address
Company phone #   Fax #   Other #
Insurance provider
Type of insurance
Policy # Group #
Company address
Company phone #   Fax #   Other #
Insurance provider
Type of insurance
Policy # Group #
Company address
Company phone #   Fax #   Other #
Insurance provider
Type of insurance
Policy # Group #
Company address
Company phone #   Fax #
Other #

Medical History Form

Name

Date of birth _____/_____/_____

HEIGHT _____   **WEIGHT** _____
Allergies (food, drug, anesthetics, or x-ray dyes)

_____

_____

_____

If yes, please list type of reaction incurred

_____

_____

_____

Current Medical Problems

Please check all current medical problems that apply from the list below:

☐ Asthma   ☐ Hiatal hernia
☐ Arthritis   ☐ Back problems
☐ Cancer   ☐ Stomach ulcer
☐ Diabetes   ☐ Bleeding problems
☐ Glaucoma   ☐ Heart disease
☐ Stroke   ☐ Depression
☐ Heart attack   ☐ Sleeping problems
☐ Cirrhosis or liver problems   ☐ Special needs
☐ Kidney problems   ☐ Participating in a study or experiment
☐ COPD   ☐ Other _____
☐ High blood pressure   _____

Profile History

Emergency contact

_____

Phone number

_____

Communication

What language do you speak? .... ☐ English   ☐ Spanish   ☐ Other

Do you read English? .... ☐ Yes   ☐ No

Do you understand English? .... ☐ Yes   ☐ No

Do you have any communication barriers?

    ☐ None   ☐ Unable to read or write

    ☐ Difficulty reading or writing   ☐ Unable to understand

Do you have hearing problems? ....☐ Yes   ☐ No

    If yes, please describe _____

Do you use any hearing devices? .... ☐ Yes   ☐ No

    If yes, please describe _____

Do you have any visual problems? .... ☐ Yes   ☐ No

    If yes, please describe _____

Do you use any vision aids? .... ☐ Yes   ☐ No

    If yes, please describe _____

Do you wear dentures? .... ☐ Yes   ☐ No

    If yes: ☐ Full   ☐ Partial

Surgical History

Have you had any previous surgeries? ....☐ Yes   ☐ No

    List all past surgeries (within past 3 years)

_____

_____

_____

_____

Vaccine History

Are your vaccinations current? .... ☐ Yes   ☐ No

Influenza .... Month/year _____/_____

Pneumonia................................... Month/year _____/_____

Tetanus2 .... Month/year _____/_____

OB-GYN History

Age of first menstrual cycle _____ **Age of onset menopause** _____

Number of pregnancies _____ **Number of children** _____

Religion

Religious preference

Do you have any cultural needs? .... ☐ Yes   ☐ No

If yes, check all that apply:

☐ Diet   ☐ Bathing

☐ Blood products   ☐ Communications

☐ Gender-specific   ☐ Other

Do you have any religious restrictions? .... ☐ Yes   ☐ No

If yes, please explain _____

Blood Transfusions

Have you had a blood transfusion? ....☐ Yes (Date _____ / _____)   ☐ No

Did you have a reaction to the transfusion? .... ☐ Yes   ☐ No

If yes, please describe reaction _____

Medical History

PSYCHOLOGICAL

Do you have any history of mental illness or treatment? . . . .☐ Yes   ☐ No
    If yes, please check all that apply:

☐ **Depression**   ☐ **Anger**
☐ **Anxiety**   ☐ **Hostility**
☐ **Panic attack**   ☐ **Tearfulness**
☐ **Stress**   ☐ **Claustrophobia**
☐ **Fatigue**   ☐ **Other**
☐ **Withdrawal**
Are you currently in treatment?   ☐ **Yes**   ☐ **No**
    Name of MD/PhD treating you for this _____
    Phone # _____
    Address _____
Have you ever felt unsafe? . . . .☐ Yes   ☐ No

In the last 6 months, have you felt like
    ☐ Harming yourself   ☐ Devising a plan to harm yourself
    ☐ Harming others

GASTROINTESTINAL HISTORY
    Check all that apply:

☐ **None**   ☐ **Difficulty chewing**
☐ **Nausea**   ☐ **Gas**
☐ **Vomiting**   ☐ **Weight loss**
☐ **Diarrhea**   ☐ **Weight gain**
☐ **Constipation**   ☐ **Decreased appetite**
☐ **Pain**   ☐ **Tenderness**
☐ **Bleeding distension**   ☐ **Cramping**
☐ **Indigestion**   ☐ **Thirst**
☐ **Difficulty swallowing**   ☐ **Change in stool**
Have you had 10% weight loss/gain in the last 6 months . . . .☐ Yes   ☐ No
    Intentional . . . .☐ Yes   ☐ No

DISEASE HISTORY

Have you had a recent infection?.................................☐ Yes   ☐ No

    Have you been exposed to an infectious disease? ....☐ Yes   ☐ No

    If yes, please list _____

Substance Use

Alcohol ....☐ Yes   ☐ No

Type:

☐ **Beer**   ☐ **Liquor**

☐ **Wine**   ☐ **Other**

    Amount/frequency per day/week _____

    Length of use_____

☐ **Days**   ☐ **Months**

☐**Weeks**   ☐**Years**

Quit date _____ / _____

Last use date _____ / _____

Tobacco...☐ Yes   ☐ No

Type:

    ☐ Cigarettes   ☐ Pipe

    ☐ Snuff/dip   ☐ Chew

    ☐ Cigar

    Amount/frequency of use # day/week_____

    Length of use # _____

    ☐ days   ☐ months

    ☐ weeks   ☐ years

Quit date _____ / _____

Are you participating in a medical research project? ....☐ Yes   ☐ No

    If yes, what? _____

    Date _____

Financials
Assets & Liabilities

Income:	
Social Security	$
Pension	$
Other	$
Assets:	$
Savings accounts	$
IRAs	$
CDs	$
Credit unions	$
Checking accounts	$
Collections	$
Investments	$
Stocks	$
Other	$
Total assets	$
Liabilities:	
Credit cards	$
Automobile	$
Real estate	$
Other	$
Total liabilities	$
Net worth	$

Financials

Monthly Expenses

Mortgage/rent	$
Utilities	$
Phone	$
Newspaper	$
Automobile	$
Groceries	$
Home maintenance	$
Home insurance	$
Life insurance	$
Cable TV	$
Medical	$
Personal care	$
Memberships	$
Other	$
Total monthly expenses	**$**

Home Medication Record

For YOUR Safety

Patient name: _____

Please list all medications you are presently taking: including prescription medications, over-the-counter medications, herbal medications, patches, ointments, injections, eye drops, inhalers

Medication name	Dosage	Medication times	Reason for taking medication	List adverse reactions

Family Medical History

▶ Maternal Grandparents

Are you adopted or unaware of your biological grandparents' medical history?. . . . .☐ Yes   ☐ No
(If yes, please move on to the Parents section.)

Grandfather's Name

Age If living	Major health problems (check all that apply) or cause of death
Age at death	☐ Cancer ☐ Diabetes ☐ Stroke ☐ Heart attack / M.I. ☐ Hypertension ☐ Other

Grandmother's Name

Age If living	Major health problems (check all that apply) or cause of death
Age at death	☐ Cancer ☐ Diabetes ☐ Stroke ☐ Heart attack / M.I. ☐ Hypertension ☐ Other

▶ Paternal Grandparents

Are you adopted or unaware of your biological grandparents' medical history?. . . . .☐ Yes   ☐ No
(If yes, please move on to the Parents section.)

Grandfather's Name

Age If living	Major health problems (check all that apply) or cause of death
Age at death	☐ Cancer ☐ Diabetes ☐ Stroke ☐ Heart attack / M.I. ☐ Hypertension ☐ Other

Grandmother's Name

Age If living	Major health problems (check all that apply) or cause of death
Age at death	☐ Cancer ☐ Diabetes ☐ Stroke ☐ Heart attack / M.I. ☐ Hypertension ☐ Other

▶ Parents

Are you adopted or unaware of your biological parents' medical history?
....☐ Yes   ☐ No

(If yes, please move on to the Brother and Sisters section.)

Father's Name

Age If living	Major health problems (check all that apply) or cause of death
	☐ Cancer ☐ Diabetes ☐ Stroke ☐ Heart attack / M.I.
Age at death	☐ Hypertension ☐ Other

Mother's Name

Age If living	Major health problems (check all that apply) or cause of death
	☐ Cancer ☐ Diabetes ☐ Stroke ☐ Heart attack / M.I.
Age at death	☐ Hypertension ☐ Other

▶ Brothers and Sisters

Are you adopted or unaware of your biological brothers' and/or sisters medical history?...☐ Yes   ☐ No

(If yes, please move on to the Children's section.)

Name   ☐ Male   ☐ Female

Age If living	Major health problems (check all that apply) or cause of death
	☐ Cancer ☐ Diabetes ☐ Stroke ☐ Heart attack / M.I.
Age at death	☐ Hypertension ☐ Other

Name   ☐ Male   ☐ Female

Age If living	Major health problems (check all that apply) or cause of death
	☐ Cancer ☐ Diabetes ☐ Stroke ☐ Heart attack / M.I.
Age at death	☐ Hypertension ☐ Other

Name   ☐ Male   ☐ Female

Age If living	Major health problems (check all that apply) or cause of death
	☐ Cancer ☐ Diabetes ☐ Stroke ☐ Heart attack / M.I.
Age at death	☐ Hypertension ☐ Other

Name ☐ Male ☐ Female

Age If living	Major health problems (check all that apply) or cause of death
Age at death	☐ Cancer ☐ Diabetes ☐ Stroke ☐ Heart attack / M.I. ☐ Hypertension ☐ Other

Name ☐ Male ☐ Female

Age If living	Major health problems (check all that apply) or cause of death
Age at death	☐ Cancer ☐ Diabetes ☐ Stroke ☐ Heart attack / M.I. ☐ Hypertension ☐ Other

▶ Children

Do you have any biological children?.............................☐ Yes   ☐ No

(If no, you have completed the Family Medical History section.)

Name ☐ Male ☐ Female

Age If living	Major health problems (check all that apply) or cause of death
Age at death	☐ Cancer ☐ Diabetes ☐ Stroke ☐ Heart attack / M.I. ☐ Hypertension ☐ Other

Name ☐ Male ☐ Female

Age If living	Major health problems (check all that apply) or cause of death
Age at death	☐ Cancer ☐ Diabetes ☐ Stroke ☐ Heart attack / M.I. ☐ Hypertension ☐ Other

Name ☐ Male ☐ Female

Age If living	Major health problems (check all that apply) or cause of death
Age at death	☐ Cancer ☐ Diabetes ☐ Stroke ☐ Heart attack / M.I. ☐ Hypertension ☐ Other

Name   ☐ Male   ☐ Female

Age If living	Major health problems (check all that apply) or cause of death
Age at death	☐ Cancer ☐ Diabetes ☐ Stroke ☐ Heart attack / M.I. ☐ Hypertension ☐ Other

Name   ☐ Male   ☐ Female

Age If living	Major health problems (check all that apply) or cause of death
Age at death	☐ Cancer ☐ Diabetes ☐ Stroke ☐ Heart attack / M.I. ☐ Hypertension ☐ Other

Name   ☐ Male   ☐ Female

Age If living	Major health problems (check all that apply) or cause of death
Age at death	☐ Cancer ☐ Diabetes ☐ Stroke ☐ Heart attack / M.I. ☐ Hypertension ☐ Other

Name   ☐ Male   ☐ Female

Age If living	Major health problems (check all that apply) or cause of death
Age at death	☐ Cancer ☐ Diabetes ☐ Stroke ☐ Heart attack / M.I. ☐ Hypertension ☐ Other

Journal

Personal Medical History

- **What medical information do I need?**

_____

_____

_____

_____

_____

_____

- **What do I need to ask other family members that isn't being recalled?**

_____

_____

_____

_____

• *What are possible sources for this information?*

_____

_____

_____

_____

_____

_____

• *Did I remember to ask family members to help with this information?*

_____

_____

_____

_____

_____

_____

_____

_____

Journal

Family Medical History

- **Who have I talked with in my family about their medical history?**

_____

_____

_____

_____

- **What information do I think I need?**

_____

_____

_____

_____

_____

_____

- *Who do I need to call?*

_____

_____

_____

_____

_____

- *Do I have my parents' and their siblings' medical history?*

_____

_____

_____

_____

_____

_____

_____

Chapter Seven

Wellness Care and Advocacy

"I must do something" always solves more problems than "something should be done."
— Author Unknown

CARING FOR A FAMILY MEMBER throughout an illness or disease is a privilege with many areas of concern. The family caregiver responsibilities and advocacy roles are key to the needs of the family member as well as the responsibilities of other providers of medical and emotional care. Without someone looking out for an ailing person, his or her care may be ineffectual and less than successful. Normally, the ailing family member will voice concerns if they are healthy, but when ill, they will be less aware of what is happening on their behalf or not alert enough to speak for themselves. This information will assist the family caregiver in understanding the resources available to aid their aging family member.

Family Caregiver Responsibilities
- Communicate with service providers—including, doctors, physician assistants, nurses, and others.

- Plan and arrange home-care services.
- File insurance claims.
- Ensure bills are paid on time.
- Address social, medical, hiring, and financial issues.
- Schedule appointments and arrange transportation for your loved one and his or her chaperone.
- Communicate with your loved one during doctor appointments and visits to the emergency room.
- Explain medical, caregiver, and financial situations to your loved one.
- Update immediate family members about your loved one's medical condition.
- Be prepared to deal with other issues as they occur.

Advocate Responsibilities

- Communicate with service providers—doctors, physician assistants, nurses, and others.
- Plan and arrange home care services.
- File insurance claims.
- Assure bills are current.
- Receive calls from loved one regarding social, medical, caregiver, and financial issues.
- Manage doctor and treatment appointments—transportation, caregiver for treatment only, and family member for doctor appointment.
- Clarify medical, caregiver, and financial situations to loved one.
- Communicate with loved one during treatment or emergency on a daily and sometime hourly basis.
- Update facility's head nurse of loved one's health status in case there is an emergency.
- Update family member of loved one's medical condition.
- Be flexible because other things not listed will occur.

Certified Nursing Assistant/Home Care Aide Responsibilities

- Be a joyful companion and a good listener.
- Assist with bathing and dressing.
- Help plan and prepare meals.
- Monitor medication.

- Monitor personal safety.
- Run errands as necessary (grocery shopping, doctor visits, etc.).
- Provide transportation as required.
- Do laundry.
- Provide incontinence care.
- Encourage physical and cognitive activities.
- Be an escort.
- Assist with walking.
- Sit with relative during hospital stays.
- Provide respite care.

Journal
Wellness Care and Advocacy

- **What are my responsibilities as a family caregiver advocate?**

_____

_____

_____

_____

_____

- **What responsibilities am I familiar with?**

_____

_____

_____

- **Which responsibilities do I need instructions on?**

_____

_____

_____

_____

• **Do I really want to be the family caregiver?**
  Who can I talk to about these duties and my concerns at this time?

_____

_____

_____

_____

• **What do I enjoy doing and will continue doing while representing the best interest of my ailing loved one?**

_____

_____

_____

_____

_____

_____

_____

_____

- *Additional notes:*

_____

_____

_____

_____

_____

_____

_____

_____

_____

_____

_____

_____

_____

Chapter Eight

Recruiting and Interviewing Caregivers

Whenever there is a human being, there is an opportunity for kindness.

— Lucius Annaeus Seneca

FINDING CAREGIVERS can be sourced from many places—friends, relatives, churches, hospital and college bulletin boards, college placement offices, institutions with classes for nursing assistants or caregivers, neighborhood newspapers, and other caregivers.

&ᖆ *Personal Experience: There were several occasions where I recruited caregivers and each time the recommending source was different. Once, a family friend heard I needed a caregiver for my mother when she lived in her home. I was told a CNA had just completed an assignment and was available. The CNA called and we scheduled to meet. After interviewing her and reviewing her credentials, I hired her to care for my mother. Eventually, I hired her daughter to cover the late night and earlier morning hours.*

Mother's health improved as she finished her chemotherapy treatment.

Seeking to hire a caregiver happened again when I needed someone to visit and assist my aunt who lived in a rehabilitation center. Because she had no children, my cousin and I were responsible for her healthcare. Almost two years after her life-changing situation, my husband retired and we relocated to the city where we planned to live after many years of working. My cousin continued to visit her after work as often as she could but someone was needed to assist my aunt and be our eyes during our absence.

A nurse at the retirement community skilled nursing area where mother lived heard I was looking for a CNA for my aunt. After speaking to the nurse about what I needed, she recommended a person who worked with her at another facility. The day I interviewed her one of my sisters was visiting and was able to be with me when I interviewed the CNA. She heard and watched her interact with rehabilitation center staff and my aunt. She was so impressed that it was suggested we hire her for Mother also. The CNA went to meet Mother and this was the beginning of a relationship that lasted until the death of my aunt and mother. Upon Mother's demise, I referred this caregiver to a friend with a loved one at the same facility where Mother lived.

CAREGIVERS KNOW OTHER CAREGIVERS and whether they are available or not. There are many advantages to hiring someone yourself:

- Your costs will be lower.
- You will determine expectations and standards.
- You will train the caregivers the way you want it done.

HOWEVER, there are disadvantages as well:

- There is no backup person to cover in the event of illness and time off.
- It takes more of your time to find the caregivers and manage the process.

BEFORE YOU INTERVIEW potential caregivers, you should make several key decisions:

- List (in detail) all the tasks you need performed; create a job description.
- Decide what you can afford to pay for wages.
- Settle on daily and weekly hours of work and scheduled time off.
- Choose your payroll cycle—when you will pay.

Caregiver Interview

USE THE FOLLOWING questions for each candidate, carefully record their answers so you can make a meaningful and informed decision about whom to hire:

- "Tell me about yourself." This open-ended question, simple as it is, can reveal a great deal about a person's character, motivation, and priorities. Look in particular for a focus on others' welfare.
- Ask applicants to describe their formal training for providing care. This will help you determine the candidate's qualifications and skills.
- Ask whether they are bonded to insure security for your home and valuable possessions. If they are not bonded, ask whether they know of any factor that might bar their bonding.
- Ask about previous care giving work experience. Ask about each applicant's length of time on the job, and the reason for leaving a job, to determine any personality conflicts and longevity on previous jobs.
- Ask the simple question, "Why do you want this job?" so you can determine a sense of commitment and dedication.
- As you discuss your needs, be aware of the would-be caregivers interjecting their view of how to do what you want and need.
- Ask about their availability and flexibility.
- Ask about their transportation to determine reliability.
- Ask about their health status to be aware of health limitations in performing your needed tasks.
- Ask for at least three employment and personal references; these should be from care-giving positions, if possible. It won't help you if they were terrific cutting hair or something not related to caregiving but were not able to provide positive references from their caregiving positions.

IF YOU DO NOT WISH to go through the hiring process yourself, call an agency that hires caregivers. There are costs associated with using an agency, but the advantage of using an agency is that someone else performs the hiring process and bears the associated risks. It can be worth the price because they manage, schedule, and pay the caregivers. All you have to do is pay the agency according to their work schedule. If the arrangement is not working well for you or your loved one, you notify the agency and the caregiver will be replaced. As a person who has engaged caregivers by both means, I recommend that when and if you become frustrated from managing the process yourself, using an agency is worth the extra cost.

Caregiver Job Description

- **Job Title:** Personal Caregiver
- **Location:** Nursing Home / Private Home

- **Job Status:** Full-Time / Part-Time
- **Job Period:** 5-day / 7-day Week

Position Overview

Provide compassionate and professional services to the client or patient, including personal grooming and hygiene support, meal preparation, vital sign monitoring, and household management. The ideal candidate will have hands-on experience and a history of success when dealing with elderly persons.

Essential Job Functions

- Assists with bathing, dressing, and personal grooming
- Plan and prepare meals
- Monitor medication
- Monitor personal safety
- Escort to medical appointments
- Collect and prepare laundry
- Provide respite care
- Provide assistance and incontinence care
- Report on status of client

Non-essential Job Functions

- Run errands as necessary (grocery shopping, doctor visits, etc.)
- Escort on outings and visits
- Assist with walking and other mobility issues
- Encourage activities

Requirements

- Loving, kind, and trustworthy
- Good communications skills
- High energy and positive attitude
- Prior example of devotion to job
- Prior caregiving work experience
- CMA / CNA welcomed, but not required

Other Skills/Abilities

- Familiarity with local area
- Manage and maneuver patient's weight
- Drive an automobile

Note: This job description is not intended to be all inclusive. Employee may perform other related duties as negotiated to meet the ongoing needs of the family.

Caregiver Schedule

Week of: _____

Day	Start Time	End Time	Total Hours	Caregiver
Monday				
Tuesday				
Wednesday				
Thursday				
Friday				
Saturday				
Sunday				
Total week hours				Primary Caregiver Signature:

Caregiver Daily Log

Date: _____

Day	Meals	Medication	Blood Pressure	Mood	Activities	Comments	Initials
Mon.							
Tues.							
Wed.							
Thurs.							
Fri.							
Sat.							
Sun.							

Caregiver Daily Log Instructions

- **Meals:** include what meals you know the person has eaten, even if you have to ask—don't guess.
- **Medication:** ask if medication has been taken, and check the pill container to be sure. Also, record what you administer.
- **Activities:** indicate what the person did while you were there, and specifically what did you do there. Write details below and/or on a blank sheet of paper.
- **Comments:** observations made during your hours. For example, the patient was a little slow; sleepy; fatigued; moody; talkative; etc.
- **Mood Scale:** (Low) 1 2 3 4 5 (High)
- **Additional details:**_____

Caregiver's Time Sheet

Patient's Name: _____

Week of:_____

Day of Week	Caregiver	Type of Work	Start Time	Stop Time	Total Hours	Rate Per Hour
APPROVED BY:						

Journal

Recruiting and Interviewing Caregivers

- **By what date do I need a caregiver to begin work?**

  Earliest: _____ Latest: _____

- **What sources do I currently have to ask about paid caregivers?**

  _____

  _____

- **What do I need to add to the suggested job description?**

  _____

  _____

  _____

  _____

  _____

- **After a week on the job, what other suggested forms need modifying to suit my situation?**

  _____

  _____

Chapter Nine

Caregiving – In the Home

In a moment of decision the best thing you can do is the right thing,
the next best thing is the wrong thing, and the worst you can do is nothing.
—Theodore Roosevelt

YOU SHOULD CONSULT your loved one's doctor about the types of housing that is suitable for your relative's recovery—for example, a rehabilitation center or in-home care.

A hospital social worker can discuss with you the Durable Power of Attorney for Health Care and the doctor's suggestions for housing options. If your loved one leaves the hospital and goes directly to a rehabilitation or skilled-nursing facility, however, he or she may qualify for financial assistance from Medicare. If the patient returns home, medical and care-giving expenses may be paid from the loved one's resources unless the physician requests home care services through Medicare. Once the Medicare allowance for a service is met and your relative's resources are depleted, you may apply for financial assistance through your state's medical assistance program.

Refer back to the information you gathered earlier regarding your loved one's medical insurance, assets, liabilities, and expenses. This information will help you make decisions for and act on behalf of the family member—especially if your relative cannot communicate clearly. *(See Chapter Six: Your Loved One's Personal Information for more details.)*

There are three basic options to consider when determining where to care for a loved one:

- ***Care given by the family in their home or in the ailing family member's home.***
- ***Care given by staff outside the home.***
- ***Care given by a family member from a far distance.***

Following is an explanation of what each of these options might entail.

Caregiving in the Home

YOU ARE THE PRIMARY FAMILY CAREGIVER and advocate for your loved one. You may choose to live in their home or move them into your home The decisions you and your loved one make will primarily involve the same home safety preparation. The major difference for the loved one living with you will involve adjusting to a new location and leaving their home. For you and your family, it is integrating your loved one into your daily family life.

Some issues the family caregiver living in the same city and local area but not living with the loved one include:

- Frequent visits and calls
- Managing the loved one's property
- Managing hired on-site caregivers who are to assist your loved one

Other differences will depend on your situation, so carefully compare and contrast options before making the final decision.

Once the decision is made you must get things done so that the care will be efficient and expedient. Other family members will help from time to time, but you are the point person who is responsible for your loved one's health and welfare. One would like this process to be simple and fast, but it takes a lot of patience and time to get things done so that you can be sure you've done your best.

Tips: For Family Caregivers

- Be kind—you'll never know how your ailing loved one is feeling, emotionally or physically.
- When you feel overwhelmed, request another family member relieve you for a few hours.
- Look for respite groups to assist you when family is unavailable.
- Create positive affirmations for yourself. *Today is a good day. I choose patience and love. I am grateful for life.*
- Get rest when your loved one naps.
- Only use the phone for a short time when caring for your loved one.
- A smile on your face, a soft touch, and laughter in your voice can cure a lot of ills. Know your limitations so that when your fuse is short you ask for help immediately.
- You are a role model for younger family members so become aware of what you are saying and doing. They are getting their training from you on taking care of you.

Preparing Your Home: Renovating and Decluttering

RENOVATION AND DECLUTTERING are the first tasks you perform before focusing more closely on providing proper personal care at home. This activity requires you to make the house friendly, safe, and accessible for your ailing family member as well as for caretakers, visitors, and you. You don't want your loved one to fall, because recovering from this injury can be traumatic for the elderly—not to mention you. As well, you should prevent falling, slipping, and tripping for yourself and visitors.

> ✄ *Personal Experience: Mother had her first knee replacement surgery three years prior to being diagnosed for multiple myeloma. In preparation for her return home from rehabilitation, several things needed restructuring and addressing at her house so that she could get around safely. A walk-in shower with handrails replaced her bathtub. A higher commode with handrail replaced the standard commode for more comfort after surgery. Doorways were widened for easy walking through with a walker and later for her wheelchair. Throw rugs were collected and removed to avoid falls. Night lights were bought and installed to illuminate dark passageways. Once the decision was made to modify her house and then, completed the work,*

Mother returned to a safer more accommodating home.

A second renovating and decluttering happened when Mother was diagnosed with multiple myeloma and received chemotherapy treatment that caused side effects requiring her to need 24/7 care. The cost of caregivers and maintaining and managing the house became unaffordable and difficult for her. There was always something at the house needing to be replaced or repaired.

The decision was made for her to move to a retirement community's independent living housing. Mother loved her house but now it was time to clear the home she and my father built sixty years ago—the house where my sisters and I had grown up. The processes for accomplishing the clearing of her house are included in the discussion in this section.

HERE ARE SEVERAL BASIC SUGGESTIONS, learned from personal experience as well as from geriatric care managers on how to make the home safe:

- Get rid of throw rugs.
- Secure carpeting and ensure it lies flat.
- Remove or remodel interior doorsills so that they are less likely to be tripping hazards.
- Improve room lighting, installing night lights for areas leading to the bathroom, especially for use at night.
- Install handrails wherever there are steps—preferably on both sides of the steps. Consider installing ramps—in some cases even where there isn't a wheelchair in the picture.
- Install grab rails on bathroom walls in the tub and the toilet areas to provide balance as one stands or sits.
- Reinstall faucet fixtures, where necessary, to ensure easy reach.
- Installing raised toilet seat with armrest will aid in keeping the person balanced while sitting or standing.
- Install adhesive-textured strips in the shower or tub to prevent falls.
- Consider placing a shower chair in the area to assist getting in and out of the tub and the shower.
- Do not wax floors—this will prevent slipping.
- Remove small items off the floor to avoid tripping and falling.

Safety

SAFETY IS AN **extremely important factor** in every home, especially when senior citizens are involved. This is true not only for the person being cared for but also for all who live or visit there. Falls are a major cause of injuries and life-changing experiences for everyone. According to Accessibility Professionals, Inc.: **"The number one risk for an independent living senior is a fall, and falls can have devastating effects. Falls account for four of every five injury-related hospitalizations by seniors. Fully, 20 percent of deaths related to an injury can be traced back to falls."**[1]

According to The U.S. National Institute on Aging (NIA): ***"Each year more than 1.6 million seniors are treated in the U.S. hospital emergency rooms for fall–related injuries caused by incidents such as slipping on a wet bathroom floor, loss of balance on stairs, or tripping on a rug."***[2]

For your ailing family member, this will not be a difficult discussion. Once they know their homes are safer, they will feel secure staying in their home or in your home, thus allowing them to be close to relatives.

Removing and reorganizing one's living space can be a volatile process. Handle it with compassion and respect. Difficult decisions will have to be made regarding treasures, keepsakes, and other accumulated collectibles. Of course, we know that "one person's trash is another person's treasures." But know, too, that there is a limit to how much a house can hold and still be safe. In some cases, a caregiver may want to include the loved one in the decision of which things to keep, which to shed, and which to put in the intermediate limbo of storage. That inclusion may give your loved one an "investment" in the process and make it more palatable. In other cases, it makes sense just to "do it," get it done for your loved one, and make "go away" a decision that would only bring more pain.

Consider the following when clearing clutter:

- **Books:** Getting rid of books can be tough for some of us. We have our favorites and ones we have read and might read again or we just haven't gotten around to reading yet. It's possible your loved one will read these books now, if physically able. You must remember that something has to be removed from the house. If you or your loved one have a lot of books, determine what books have out of date information or are not the sort of material your loved one now enjoys. Knowing how to do this may be tricky, so do get some help. Suggestions and or instructions on how to do it yourself can be found in your public library.

1 Accessibility Professionals. *Home Safety for Seniors,* Niagara Falls, NY, 21 09
2 Ibid.

Check with your loved one to see whether a book has any other meaningful reason not to be given away, such as its being author-autographed, written by a family member or a friend, etc. Always ask for their opinion, if possible. While they may not agree at this moment, they will frequently decide on their own to tell you when it can be thrown away.

- **Kitchen cabinets and counter space:** While this may not seem important, the space you create in cabinets can house items now lying about on the counters, tables, and other places you'll need to keep clear for medical and other needs. Kitchen cabinets may contain spices and other items unused for years and dried food products that could be infested with vermin or other contaminants. Clear out kitchen cabinets thoroughly, shelf paper and all, and vacuum these out before restocking. Old, small household appliances that are broken or not used but take up space can be thrown away or donated to a worthy cause.

- **Bathrooms and medications:** The bathroom often is the location for a medicine cabinet filled with medicines beyond their expiration dates. Unused, expired, or no longer needed medication should be thrown away safely. Medicine without an expiration date should be tossed away unless you know it was purchased within the past year. If it has been in a warm, moist bathroom cabinet, it has probably lost its effectiveness in any event. *An example of this is the antibiotic tetracycline. If taken when out of date, it can cause kidney failure.*

  Previously, we flushed old medication down the toilet to avoid children and animals from finding them in the garbage. However, today the Environmental Protection Agency recommends against this, to protect our sewage plants, water, fish and wildlife.

  Drug abuse is another reason for expired or unused medication to be discarded properly. Your pharmacist will guide you on how to clear the house of these medications. Get to know your pharmacists. They can be an excellent source for what and how to do a lot of things as you care for your loved one.

- **Paths and walkway:** Paths in living areas such as the bedroom, living room, and den should be free of extra furniture, plants, accessories, and the like.

- **Basement:** Cleaning out the basement is similar to decluttering other areas of the house. Use boxes and plastic containers to help make the sorting process easier. Create appropriate labels for the containers—trash, donate, sell, and recycle. Now look for items that are appropriate for each container. Examine old toys, tools, and electronics to determine whether they still work. Save the working ones for an estate or garage sale.

The raw materials (lead, mercury and cadmium, are a few examples) in electronic waste can become carcinogens if not disposed of properly. So put them aside to be transported to the appropriate recycle center. Look in your local city telephone directory to locate the proper recycling center for this material.

In the case of flammable items such as paint, old household cleaning products, pesticides. and other liquids you aren't sure about, box them up and take to the local flammable materials collection site. Your city's trash collection department or any waste management firm can advise.

For items remaining in the basement, store them in labeled plastic containers, stacked in an organized way so that they can be found when you need them.

- **Linen closets:** Worn and discolored towels, sheets, and other household items, including paper and clothes, get stored and forgotten in linen closets. Once these are sorted, you may find that you need new linens or that you have too many unusable ones.

- **Under the bed:** This is a great hiding place for most people. Things could have been hidden there and forgotten. Now this is a place for household pests, dirt, and dust. These are not the best things to have around anyone—especially a person needing medical care.

- **Garage:** A garage is often a prime pathway in and out of the house. Old items like paint, household products, tools, and lawn equipment find their way out of the house and into our garages. Some products can be carcinogenic or flammable, and therefore dangerous for anyone, but especially for the sick and elderly. Containers with gasoline, barbecue lighter fluid, kerosene fuel, old paint and batteries, and motor oil are potential causes of spontaneous combustion. Old newspapers and magazines, clothes, and oily rags are fuel for fires. Don't forget the old bug repellent that years ago contained DDT. Your local fire department can help you learn how to throw out flammable items. Usually they will advise you how and where to safely dispose of hazardous materials and will sometimes take materials away for you.

Throw away old items no longer being used and find a place for everything you keep. If you have it organized, tripping over it won't occur and you can find it when you need it. Most of all you, will not have to buy it again.

Tips: Decluttering

- Get an estimate for hiring someone to declutter. The price will motivate you to do it with a smile.
- Allow yourself at least one hour to get organized.
- Get someone to help you.
- Establish a timeline for completing the job.
- Do one room at a time so it won't be overwhelming.
- Gift items and you will feel better about getting rid of them.
- Clean a drawer or shelf at a time.

How to discard items

ONCE YOU KNOW what to get rid of, you must determine what to do with it. You have several options:

- Sell or give to family and friends after first asking the owner.
- Donate to a charity thrift shop.
- If it looks valuable, take the item or a photograph of it to an antique appraiser.
- Rent a Dumpster.
- Call your city's trash department for their policy and schedule for trash pick up.
- Call your local law enforcement department for directions on what to do with guns and ammunition.
- Take clothing apparel to a consignment shop but call first for their policy for accepting items.
- Conduct an estate sale.

If an estate sale is your choice, call at least three auctioneers to gain an idea of their procedures, process and terms. Make sure that the auctioneer you engage is duly licensed for the state in which the auction will be held, and for the kind of auction to be held—in some jurisdictions, for example, an auction house needs a special license or endorsement if an estate sale is to include real property.

DECLUTTERING A HOUSE can be an emotional experience. Items are discovered and rediscovered from many years ago—when you were a young child or times that cause your loved one, or you yourself, to relive a good or not so good emotional experience. Sometimes it helps to discuss these experiences with others to share your perception of things you could not see as a child. This may also help you and the loved one bring closure to some situations. Be patient as you get through these times, because it is hard to let go of items or issues that generate memories.

Home Safety and Security

ANOTHER METHOD of ensuring a safe home environment is to subscribe to an electronic surveillance service. If there is a security system in the home, the company may already have a service that can be added for personal emergency needs. With most of these services, a personal help button comes in either a waterproof wristband or a pendant. If the loved one has an emergency, they push the help button that is connected to a trained professional through a two-way voice intercom. If they are not near the base to respond, help will be sent automatically on their behalf.

> One company that provides this service is ADT. Search their website for more information. You'll find others as well on the Internet, and it's wise to do some comparison-shopping.
>
> Another company that provides a medical alert service is Philips Lifeline. They also offer bracelets and necklaces engraved with your primary medical conditions, an ID number, and 24-hour emergency response center number. This company can also be found on the Internet.

The next eye opening, time consuming, emotional, and important step is ACTION. Once you have determined what has to be done to the home to accommodate your loved one's needs, arrange meetings with several renovation companies to get estimates of cost and a time frame for the project. I suggest you call local agencies like the Health Department that can give you information, or send someone to give you on-site advice and the names of other agencies to make suggestions.

Whatever changes you make must be convenient for the loved one and for you. Look for recommended firms and sources for financing the project through local agencies or family members.

Journal

Caregiving - In the Home

- **What care does my loved one need?**

_____

_____

_____

_____

_____

_____

- **What are the "Pros" and "Cons" of an Assisted Living Facility for my loved one?**

Pros: _____

_____

_____

Cons: _____

_____

_____

• **What are the "Pros" and "Cons" of a Skilled Nursing Facility for my loved one?**

Pros:

_____

_____

_____

Cons:

_____

_____

_____

_____

• **How do I feel about participating in this decision?**

_____

_____

_____

• **What family member or friend do I feel comfortable discussing this decision with?**

_____

_____

_____

- *Additional notes:*

_____

_____

_____

_____

_____

_____

_____

_____

_____

_____

_____

_____

_____

Chapter Ten

Assisted Living Facility

May He give you the desire of your heart and make all your plans succeed.
— Psalm 20:4

TO FIND THE PROPER CAREGIVING SITUATION outside the home, you will have to research to find what will fit your situation. What you want to know first is what you need in terms of care. The doctor or hospital will tell you what is necessary for your loved one to recover or to be maintained. The two primary housing options for your loved one's needs are Assisted Living and Skilled Nursing Care facilities. However, this choice will be based on their medical needs.

Assisted Living

IF YOUR LOVED ONE may return home but managing the house and their care is difficult, consider moving them to an assisted living facility. This is a residential option that provides independence, and helps with healthcare and daily activities. This housing choice gives your loved one the residential setting and the chance to be with others for meals and social activities. The main focus is providing an environment that supports good health and connection to family.

> ❧ *Personal Experience of a Relative: There came a time in my dad's life when making reasonable decisions and judgments about his safety and health were no longer in his capacity to do. Medicines were too easily forgotten, and open flames on a gas stove became a better warming option than increasing the temp on the thermostat. Dad's medicines were multiple; this was inclusive of a series of eye drops to be used at alternating intervals, to offset the onset of glaucoma. I didn't know what to expect from one day to the next, as my siblings and I grew less capable of maintaining a twenty-four hour watch for our only remaining parent. As He often does, God granted us the wisdom to pursue an assisted living facility to provide the care our father obviously needed, which we could not give, no matter how much we loved him.*
>
> *Ultimately, the peace and contentment of knowing that even in the privacy of his own one-bedroom apartment, Dad was afforded a continuum of care and companionship beyond the scope of his family's capability. In retrospect, it seems that Dad had more visitors and interaction with close friends and family while residing in his assisted living apartment than the last few years he spent in his own house. These were happy visits, as I remember them, which enhanced Dad's quality of life and emotional tranquility, while improving his overall health.*

OTHER NAMES USED to refer to assisted living establishments are *community residences, personal care homes, residential care communities,* and *adult congregate living communities.* The central theme of these locations is to enrich an elderly person's life in a community setting.

The residents share amenities offered while having the pleasure to come and go as much as they desire. Of course, this is based on the resident's capability to be mobile. The cost varies based on the community, living space, and selected services chosen or needed.

To locate an assisted living community that's right for your loved one, view the Assisted Living Federation Association (ALFA) website, or contact the Eldercare Locator at 1-800-677-1116 or your local area Agency on Aging.

The ALFA provides a checklist for assessing assisted living communities. It covers the facility's environment, physical features, medication and health care, services and amenities, individual apartment features, social recreational activities, food and other questions. Take with you the Assisted Living Checklist outlined in this chapter and use the visitation techniques discussed under *Skilled Nursing Care* in Chapter Eleven.

- ***Trust yourself:*** If an observation is made, then ask the person touring with you to observe and listen closely to how they answer you. If the staff member should fail to answer or volunteer to obtain the information, ask to speak to the staff member who would know. Be persistent but courteous and gentle. You are interested, ultimately, not in assurances, but in learning what the real standards are.

  If you feel comfortable in the facility, your loved one will be fine, once the person adjusts to the change. These facilities are regulated by the State's Health Services Department. If there are concerns that can't be resolved with local administration, call this agency for directions on filing a complaint.

- ***Arrive early:*** Well before your appointment time, wait in the lobby. Just watch and listen to the interaction of residents, staff, and visiting families. Most residents and staff will speak to you. It is an opportunity for you to ask a few questions. At a minimum, ask the following questions:
  - » Are you a resident?
  - » How long have you been here?
  - » Do you like living here?
  - » What do you like most?
  - » What do you like least?

Their initial reaction will give you the best barometer of the facility. If you talk with a family member, ask similar questions. Then follow with "If you had to do it again, would you select this facility?"

While touring, you will possibly meet the facility's director. Questions for this person could include:

- Why should our family choose this facility?
- What is your most challenging issue in dealing with residents?
- Who are your competitors?

The answers you get may not discourage you from selecting the facility, but they will give you a view of how involved, how knowledgeable, and how open the administration is.

ON ONE OF YOUR VISITS, you will see the residents' area. Please do not judge the facility by the entrance. They all have wonderful entrance areas, which sometime belie what's beyond, masking the type of care the residents actually receive. Here are some of the key observations you should make.

- **Residents:** Residents should appear clean and dressed for daytime activities, with staff dressing professionally for work and wearing visible identification badges.
- **Interactions:** The interaction of staff, residents and visitors should be friendly and respectful. Staff should communicate in a professional, friendly manner at all times.
- **Safety features:** Should be apparent throughout the building and in the residents' private living spaces—smoke detectors, rails in bathrooms, handicap ramps, and walk-in or step-in showers.
- **Call buttons, intercom, or telephone:** Better yet, two or more of these, should provide immediate access to staff. Emergencies do happen, so observe whether a staff member appears present at all times. For example, is there a receptionist always on duty?
- **Storage:** Space should be available for all residents, easy to access and secure. Your loved one's belongings should be stored where you and your loved one can get to them with reasonable convenience.
- **Layout of rooms:** Should be spacious, attractive, and uncluttered, leaving room for safe movement of residents, visitors, and staff. Changes and new environments are awkward for loved ones coming from homes they've known for years. Open areas are safer and easier to get used to.

NOW THAT YOU and your loved one have decided on a housing option outside the home, you must next determine whether or not to sell the family home. If their situation requires the house to be sold, you should call a few Realtors® for their suggestions, comments and recommended asking price. Don't rush into this unless it is an essential step and there is no possibility your loved one will ever return home. The next task is clearing and possibly renovating areas of the house. While you are making the decision of which Realtor to use, start discussions regarding clearing items out of the house with the input of your loved one and their extended family. This is a big job, but if organized properly it may be completed in a short period of time. Refer back to *Renovating and Decluttering, and Discarding Items* in Chapter Nine for suggested techniques that are appropriate for your situation.

Assisted Living Checklist

Name of nursing home:
_____

Date of visit:
_____

General inquiry	
Is there a contract describing admission and discharge policies, fees, and services?	☐ Yes ☐ No
Is this contract available for you to read before you have to make a decision?	☐ Yes ☐ No
Are rooms private?	☐ Yes ☐ No
Is there a special Alzheimer's care area?	☐ Yes ☐ No
Can residents choose their doctor and pharmacy?	☐ Yes ☐ No
Is there a care plan for residents?	☐ Yes ☐ No
Are pets allowed?	☐ Yes ☐ No
What shared areas are available?	
What special services are available?	

Observation visits	
Is the facility in a convenient location to you?	☐ Yes ☐ No
Is the facility clean and cheerful?	☐ Yes ☐ No
Do you get a good feeling about the facility?	☐ Yes ☐ No
Is the staff appropriately dressed?	☐ Yes ☐ No
Does staff interact with each other and residents in a professional and friendly manner?	☐ Yes ☐ No
Is the facility smoke free?	☐ Yes ☐ No
Are stairs and halls well lit?	☐ Yes ☐ No
Is the floor plan logical?	☐ Yes ☐ No
Are there optional floor plans?	☐ Yes ☐ No
Is the floor space adequate for the resident's needs?	☐ Yes ☐ No
Do rooms and bathrooms have handrails and call buttons?	☐ Yes ☐ No
Are kitchens in the resident's unit?	☐ Yes ☐ No
Are there security and fire safety systems?	☐ Yes ☐ No
Is there an emergency alternate power source?	☐ Yes ☐ No
Healthcare services	
What healthcare services are provided?	☐ Yes ☐ No
Are social and recreational activities available?	☐ Yes ☐ No
Is assistance available "24/7"?	☐ Yes ☐ No
What meals are included?	☐ Yes ☐ No
Where are meals served?	☐ Yes ☐ No
Are housekeeping, linen and personal laundry services provided?	☐ Yes ☐ No
Are there furnished units?	☐ Yes ☐ No

Can residents come and go at will?	☐ Yes ☐ No
Are transportation services available? Where?	☐ Yes ☐ No
Are visitors welcomed at all times?	☐ Yes ☐ No
Is there parking for residents? If yes, is there a parking fee?	☐ Yes ☐ No
Is visitor parking available?	☐ Yes ☐ No
Staffing	
Are there state requirements for staff?	☐ Yes ☐ No
Do they meet state requirements?	☐ Yes ☐ No
Has the facility ever been cited for falling short of state requirements? If yes, ask for an explanation.	☐ Yes ☐ No
What is the professional background of administrators of the facility?	☐ Yes ☐ No
Does staff meet with family representatives as needed or as requested by family?	☐ Yes ☐ No
Costs	
Is there an entrance fee? If so, how much is it?	☐ Yes ☐ No
Is there a monthly rent?	☐ Yes ☐ No
Is there a deposit? If so, is it refundable?	☐ Yes ☐ No
What utilities are included?	☐ Yes ☐ No
What is the history of rate increases?	☐ Yes ☐ No
Is there a charge for late payment?	☐ Yes ☐ No
What happens when the resident's funds are depleted?	☐ Yes ☐ No
If hospitalization or a nursing home stay is required, how long is unit held for the resident?	No. of days

Journal

Assisted Living

- **What care does my loved one need?**

_____

_____

_____

- **What are the "Pros" and "Cons" of an assisted living facility for my loved one?**

Pros:
_____

_____

_____

Cons:
_____

_____

_____

- **What are the "Pros" and "Cons" of a skilled nursing facility for my loved one?**

Pros:
_____

_____

_____

Cons:

_____

_____

_____

_____

- ***How do I feel about participating in this decision?***

_____

_____

_____

_____

_____

- ***What family members or friends do I feel comfortable discussing this decision with?***

_____

_____

_____

_____

_____

• *What assisted living facility staff should I contact?*

#1 Name of facility:
_____

_____

Pros:
_____

_____

_____

_____

Cons:
_____

_____

_____

_____

Contact 1 Information:
_____

Position:
_____

_____

Contact 2 Information:
_____

_____

Do I have their business card? ☐ *Yes* ☐ *No*

Notes:
_____

_____

_____

#2 Name of facility:

Pros:

Cons:

Contact 1 Information:

Position:

Contact 2 Information:

Do I have their business card? ☐ Yes ☐ No

Notes:

#3 Name of facility:

_____

_____

Pros: _____

_____

_____

Cons: _____

_____

_____

Contact 1 Information: _____

Position: _____

_____

Contact 2 Information: _____

_____

- *Do I have their business card?* ☐ *Yes* ☐ *No*

Notes: _____

_____

Chapter Eleven

Nursing Homes and Skilled Nursing Facilities

Faith makes all things possible; love makes all things easy.
—Author Unknown

IF YOUR LOVED ONE'S CONDITION requires more skilled care than can be provided at home or at an assisted living residence, you will need to find qualified rehabilitation and healthcare facilities, also known as skilled nursing facilities and nursing homes. Determining the right facility for your relative is difficult, and it will take time to get it right. Knowing the details of your relative's financial assets, liabilities, and medical insurance coverage will help you determine the best place for your loved that falls within their budget.

While your loved one is in the hospital, a social worker can give you a list of sites. Narrow these options down to three or four places that satisfy your concerns about location, affordability, and reputation. Next, schedule visits to these facilities and take along a family member or friend as a second pair of eyes and ears. Once you have the list of facilities that you want to consider, prepare a checklist for each of them so that you know what you are looking for before you make the visit. *(See Nursing Home Checklist at the end of this chapter.)*

> ❧ **Personal Experience:** *The Medicare checklist came in very handy when Mother was spending her life savings for around-the-clock caregivers. It was decided that I would look for housing where Mother could move and costs were more affordable. A friend had just gone through this process for her husband. She shared her short list of places she liked and I started my search and investigation. I first drove in the neighborhood where they were located to assess their convenience for me and other visitors. I narrowed the list down and visited unannounced. After these visits, the list included only three facilities and appointments were arranged to tour them.*
>
> *The facility needed to have different levels of health care so as Mother aged relocating her wasn't necessary. This brought the list to two facilities. On my second visit, I took my checklist and proceeded to closely evaluate them. One retirement community met the majority of the needs—affordable, very pleasant, friendly, and four levels of housing. My sisters and Mother went to visit the facility and we all thought it ideal for Mother to apply for admission. Mother agreed to proceed but you could tell she was cautiously optimistic about this move. The admission board approved Mother's application after reviewing a significant amount of personal and financial information. Eventually, she became excited about moving, and she lived there until her death.*

> ❧ **Personal Experience:** *A year after Mother moved to the retirement community, my aunt was hospitalized. She needed around the clock medical care and, therefore, needed to be dismissed from the hospital directly to a rehabilitation center. My cousin and I were given a list of facilities to determine a suitable one for her. Well, the Medicare Checklist and experience from Mother's situation helped us make this choice. Since my cousin worked, I visited places I had selected during the day, and she would visit on the weekends. We scheduled another visit for a closer evaluation of our best choice facility. The hospital social worker was given our selection and sought her admission. My aunt was transferred there and lived there for the rest of her life.*

YOUR SITE VISITS won't reveal all of a facility's shortcomings—you won't become aware of some of them until your loved one is living there. However, your relative's care will be enhanced if you visit the facility often and persistently advocate for him or her. Ask staff—including medical, social work and business office—questions about things you observe. Remember to document all conversations for future reference—including date, staff person's name, and issue discussed.

Some facilities invite a resident's family members to quarterly meetings to discuss concerns. It's important that you attend these meetings. Listen attentively to issues brought up by your loved one or staff persons and voice any concerns you may have. Also, pay close attention to what family members of other residents say about the facility. Hearing their concerns will give you knowledge about things to look for and to avoid.

Although quarterly meetings are a good venue for you to address issues about your relative's care, there may be times when you'll need to request special meetings with the facility's director or administrators. For example, if a problem recurs after you've discussed it with the staff providing direct care to your loved one, you'll want to meet with the management about it before your anger and frustration build. It's difficult to stay calm, clear and respectful when you feel that your loved one is being neglected or harmed. Therefore, prepare for all meetings. Bring a list of your concerns and support them with documentation from previous staff discussions.

> Remember, your relative can no longer represent himself or herself as effectively as you can.

Nursing Home Checklist

Name of nursing home:

Date of visit:

	Yes	No	Comments
Basic information			
The nursing home is Medicare certified.			
The nursing home is Medicaid certified.			
The nursing home has the level of care you need (e.g., skilled, custodial), and a bed is available.			
The nursing home offers training and continuing education programs for all staff.			
The nursing home has special services, if needed, in a separate unit (e.g., dementia, ventilator, or rehabilitation), and a bed is available.			
The nursing home is close enough for friends and family to visit.			
Residents' appearance	**Yes**	**No**	**Comments**
Residents are clean, appropriately dressed for the season or time of day, and well groomed.			
Nursing home living spaces	**Yes**	**No**	**Comments**
The nursing home is free from overwhelming, unpleasant odors.			
The nursing home appears clean and well kept.			
The temperature in the nursing home is comfortable for residents.			
The nursing home has good lighting.			

	Yes	No	Comments
Noise levels in the dining room and other common areas are comfortable.			
Smoking isn't allowed or is restricted to certain areas of the nursing home.			
Furnishings are sturdy yet comfortable and attractive.			
Staff	**Yes**	**No**	**Comments**
The relationship between the staff and the residents appears to be warm, polite and respectful.			
All personnel wear name badges.			
Staff members knock on the door before entering a resident's room and refer to residents by name.			
The nursing home offers training and continuing education programs for all staff.			
The nursing home does background checks on all staff.			
The guide on your tour knows the residents by name and is recognized by them.			
There are licensed nurses present 24 hours a day, including a registered nurse at least 8 hours per day, 7 days a week.			
The same team of nurses and CNAs work with the same residents 4 to 5 days per week.			
CNAs work with a reasonable number of residents.			
CNAs are involved in care-planning meetings.			
A full-time social worker is on staff.			

	Yes	No	Comments
A licensed doctor is present at the facility daily and can be reached at all times.			
The nursing home's management team (including the director of nursing and the administrator) has worked together for at least one year.			
What does the facility do when it is short staffed? For example, does it skip baths?			
Residents' Rooms	**Yes**	**No**	**Comments**
Residents may have personal belongings and furniture in their rooms. What are the limits?			
Each resident has storage space (closet and drawers) in his or her room.			
Is there extra onsite storage?			
Each resident has a window in his or her bedroom.			
Each resident has a window in his or her bedroom.			
Residents have access to a personal telephone and television.			
Residents have a choice of roommates.			
Residents can reach water pitchers and individually adjustable temperature controls.			
Hallways, stairs, lounges, and bathrooms	**Yes**	**No**	**Comments**
Exits are clearly marked.			
There are quiet areas where residents can visit with friends and family.			
The nursing home has smoke detectors and sprinklers.			

	Yes	No	Comments
All common areas, resident rooms and doorways are designed for wheelchair use.			
There are handrails in the hallways and grab bars in the bathrooms.			
Light switches are accessible to disabled residents.			
Menus and Food	**Yes**	**No**	**Comments**
Residents have a choice of food items at each meal. (Ask if your loved one's favorite foods are served.)			
The nursing home can accommodate dietary requirements—diabetes, kosher foods, and nuts and other allergy-related issues.			
Nutritious snacks are available upon request.			
Staff helps residents eat and drink at mealtimes, if help is needed.			
Activities	**Yes**	**No**	**Comments**
Residents, including those who are bound to their rooms, may choose to take part in a variety of activities.			
The nursing home has outdoor areas for resident use and staff helps residents to go outside.			
Safety and care	**Yes**	**No**	**Comments**
The nursing home has an emergency evacuation plan and holds regular fire drills (bed-bound residents included).			
Residents get preventive care, such as a yearly flu shot, to help keep them healthy.			
Residents may still see their personal doctors.			

	Yes	No	Comments
The nursing home has an arrangement with a nearby hospital and ambulance service for emergencies.			
Care plan meetings are held with residents and family members at convenient times whenever possible.			
The nursing home has corrected all deficiencies on its last state inspection report. (Ask to see the report.)			

Journal
Nursing Homes and Skilled Nursing Care

- **What type of medical care does my loved one need?**

_____

_____

_____

_____

- **What is my attitude towards nursing homes?**

_____

_____

_____

_____

- **What makes the nursing home different from the skilled nursing care facility for my loved one?**

_____

_____

_____

- *What can I do to soften the stereotype of a nursing home to my loved one?*

_____

_____

_____

- *What nursing homes and skilled nursing care staff should I contact?*

#1 Facility Name: _____

_____

Staff Contact: _____

Position: _____

_____

Contact Information: _____

_____

_____

- *Do I have their business cards?* ☐ *Yes*   ☐ *No*

Notes: _____

_____

_____

#2 Facility Name:

_____

Staff Contact: _____

Position: _____

_____

Contact Information: _____

_____

_____

- ***Do I have their business cards?*** ☐ *Yes* ☐ *No*

Notes: _____

_____

_____

_____

_____

#3 Facility Name:

Staff Contact:

Position:

Contact Information:

- ***Do I have their business cards?* ☐ *Yes*   ☐ *No***

Notes:

Chapter Twelve

Caregiving From a Distance

Do not let them out of your sight, keep them within your heart.
— Proverbs 4:21

ACCORDING TO THE FAMILY CAREGIVER ALLIANCE, a national advocacy group supporting caregiver needs, services and information, many families are providing caregiving to elderly family members from a far distance.[1] Families are spread out across the country; they live where employment takes them and leave their loved ones in the area where they were born. Many of you may have to make similar decisions, as I did. This means you must consider how to provide healthcare for an elderly loved one who does not live nearby. After discussing the situation with your loved one, offer them the choice of relocating to live with you or moving to another location where there are supportive family members. In most cases an elderly person will opt to stay where they live—familiarity with the area, local friendships, and memberships in churches and other

1 Family Caregiver Alliance. National Center on Caregiving, *www.caregiver.org*

organizations are powerful motivators. Once you have talked through this option and the decision has been made for your loved one stay where they are, you must determine the best way to oversee their health care from a distance.

> ❧ **Personal Experience:** *Once the decision was made for my husband and me to relocate to our retirement home in another city, I asked my mother and my aunt did they want to move with us. They wanted to remain in the city they had lived all their lives. This was discussed a few times in case they had changed their minds.*
>
> *In preparation for our relocating to a far distance from loved ones I was the primary caregiver for, plans needed to be made regarding who was to watch over them in my absence. With my mother, my sisters who lived out of town agreed to share with me alternately coming back each month to take mother to her doctor appointments and to check on our aunt.*
>
> *The aunt was in a rehabilitation center that provided her constant medical care so I wasn't too concerned. However, I began to realize medical care was not the only thing needed to help her be happy and live the best life she could live. She needed companionship and familiar faces visiting and caring about her. My cousin provided what she could because she worked all week, but other times needed covering. I also needed the facility to know there was someone visiting her regularly during my absence.*
>
> *This was when the caregiver was hired who was with her until her death. As was mentioned earlier, this caregiver was also the loyal, dedicated person who cared for my mother until her death. Besides hiring the caregiver, there were constant telephone calls to and from the nurse's station reporting concerns and giving updates on her medical status.*

Being an advocate for any loved one's health care is a continuing challenge. Being the primary overseer of this care from a far distance is many times more demanding and frustrating for several reasons.

You only have direct contact with an ailing loved one via landline or cellular telephone communications. Some cell phones are difficult for an elderly person to hear with, especially if the person needs a hearing device. Both ends of the communication can be deceiving because voice alone does not allow you to have the best understanding of the person's physical and emotional state. What is more important, the loved one may forget and not tell you, or you may forget to ask about key critical events. You cannot have visual access to the situation, which causes additional concern. You must give directions and make decisions without complete information. All information one gets is from the loved one who may not be objective. The voice connection raises yet another concern—you will not be able to observe, as you could if physically present, when a loved one is experiencing fatigue, depression, weight loss, diminished appetite, or other such symptoms.

The caregiver working from a distance will have to travel to see the loved one. Taking time off or family leave from a job to travel by car, plane, or train can add strain to one's budget, work life, and immediate family. These visits can sometimes be planned, but not all of the time as health can change suddenly in anyone who is ailing. If you are retired and on a fixed income you may have to make extreme sacrifices to be able to afford travel that is not scheduled in advance.

Sharing the responsibility with siblings living in remote locations can be problematic. This option is present when the only immediate family member in the area has to relocate. If there are other siblings who are willing to share the long distance care giving responsibilities, this can help to ease the duties of the primary caregiver. At the least, ask a distant relative in the local area to make frequent visits to see the loved one, if possible.

Close friends of the loved one who volunteer to become a part of the healthcare team may be in for a rude awakening. Seek your loved one's approval first before making the decision to include others. While a friend's inclusion can be a wonderful idea, be mindful of its limitations—the friend's lack of complete knowledge of medical history and present condition, time available for this task, the friend's own personal and family situation, and their ability to do as you would do for your relative are all sources of uncertainty. The special connection blood relatives have—a connection that generally does not exist with friendships—is unique. Friends may feel they have a closer relationship to the loved one than do their relatives since they are close by. But when the worst behavior rears its head and the loved one is ailing, in pain, and perhaps behaving differently, a friend sees them in a different light. Relatives will overlook such behavior, but asking a friend to forgive and forget it may be an unrealistic expectation. Keep this "connectivity factor" in mind as you make any decision to have a friend act in your stead.

Consider hiring a Geriatric Care Manager to monitor and manage the health care of your loved one. They have professional nursing experience and can perform many of these services instead of you. A hospital social worker, senior services agency, doctor's office, or an Internet search for the National Professional Association of Geriatric Care Managers should provide a list of companies in your area for you to consider.

Making the decision to oversee a loved one's health care from a distance can be an adventure in itself. The process will provide you with additional information and insight into agencies, businesses, individuals, and groups eager to help and guide you to the right decision that works for your situation and for your loved one.

Anticipatory Grief

Your grieving process begins the day you learn that a loved one has been told that he or she has a terminal illness. The psychological term for this is anticipatory grief. During this stage, you may experience the following symptoms:

- Insomnia
- Irritability
- Impaired concentration
- Change in appetite
- Change in weight
- Frequent negative thinking
- Fatigue
- Disorganization

Anticipatory grief is magnified when you are responsible for caregiving for a loved one and live at a distance.

See Chapter Fifteen: Taking Care of Yourself *to better understand how to help yourself by getting help.*

Journal
Caregiving From a Distance

- **What concerns me about being away from my ailing loved one?**

_____

_____

_____

_____

_____

_____

- **How can I address these concerns?**

_____

_____

_____

_____

_____

_____

_____

• **What concerns are out of my control?**

_____

_____

_____

_____

_____

_____

• **What professional individuals and/or organizations can help me deal with these concerns?**

_____

_____

_____

_____

_____

I,_____ , promise to do my best for my loved one from a distance.

Chapter Thirteen

Smooth Transitions

When it is obvious that the goal cannot be reached,
don't adjust the goal, adjust the action steps.
— Confucious

THE TIME MAY COME when your loved one needs to move outside their home or your home because of the need for more care. The transition from home is difficult for loved ones and their adult children because they have to let go of the memories, including the family home. In addition, it is difficult for them to break strong ties to people and services in their community. They are familiar and comfortable with their established daily routine, and leaving these behind may be disturbing and create stressful feelings. Keep in mind that during this time loved ones have a sense of losing their independence. Believe it or not, your loved one will adjust to their new environment and will indicate they should have done it sooner.

To assist you in making this transition smoother for them and you, here are some suggestions. If the idea of moving is still objectionable to them or it is having an emotional and physical impact upon them, notify their primary care physician immediately.

Another professional with expertise in situations like these is the social worker at the facility where they are moving. Their job is to help your loved one and their family with difficult situations such as this. The physician and the facility's staff are available to assist you, but you must inform them of your need for their help.

Tips: Making a Smooth Transition

- Initiate communication early.
- Be patient and gentle.
- Discuss situation with family members.
- Respect loved one's perspective.
- Give them tasks.
- Maintain some of the loved one's autonomy.
- Be sensitive to loved ones maintaining their empowerment by letting them make choices and try not to take away their sense of control over their lives.
- Take memorable items and photographs.
- Go slow to allow time for adjusting emotionally.
- Hire movers or ask the family to assist with the move.

Journal
Smooth Transitions

- **What are some of your favorite memories of your relationship with your loved one?**

_____

_____

_____

_____

_____

- **What are some of your favorite memories of your loved one's home?**

_____

_____

_____

_____

_____

- *How will you use these memories to ease the transition of your loved one to a new home?*

_____

_____

_____

_____

_____

- *Who (family member or non-family member) can help you with this transition?*

_____

_____

- *Additional notes:*

_____

_____

_____

_____

_____

Chapter Fourteen

Caregiver and Loved One Abuse

*How far you go in life depends on your being tender with the young,
compassionate with the aged, sympathetic with the striving and tolerant of the weak and
strong. Because someday in your life you will have been all of these.*
— George Washington Carver

ACCORDING TO the *New England Journal of Medicine,* between one and two million older Americans experience mistreatment in a year.[1] Elder abuse occurs when an individual is vulnerable to mistreatment because they are not able to protect themselves. Mistreatment is categorized as physical, emotional or psychological, sexual, neglect or abandonment, and financial or exploitive.[2] This mistreatment often occurs when the caregiver becomes overwhelmed or burdened with the duties of caregiving in addition to the stresses of everyday living.

Caregiver abuse may occur in the home as well as in other environments where older

1 Lachs, Mark S., M.D., M.P.H. and Karl Pillemar, Ph.D. *New England Journal of Medicine,* 1995; 332: 437-443. February 16, 1995.
2 Ebersole et al., 2008.

adults receive care such as assisted living facilities and nursing homes. For many of us this sounds like an unfortunate situation, but it happens every day. It is critical for you to become aware and remain vigilant so mistreatment or abuse won't happen at all.

ABUSE BY CAREGIVERS in the home will become immediately apparent because you will observe physical evidence such as bruises, cuts, an unkempt family member, behavioral changes in the loved one or the like, and you may also hear of improper caregiver behaviors or complaints from the family member.

In an assisted living facility, there will be fewer problems like these because the family member is better able to care for themselves. However, if they complain about medicine not being administered in a timely or appropriate manner, their living space not kept clean, or neglect or lack of other provided services, report it to the facility's administrative staff immediately. Take your family member's complaints seriously and investigate them. Sometimes their imagination may be creative but you will discover the truth as you investigate and ask questions of the administrative staff and your loved one.

Some of the visible signs of abuse in a nursing home that should be investigated are:

- Resident being kept in an over-medicated state.
- Bedsore or frozen joints.
- Torn, stained or bloody underwear; vaginal or anal bleeding; unexplained venereal disease or genital infection.
- Sudden change in behavior.
- Loss of resident's possessions.
- Unexplained bruises, cuts, burns, sprains, or fractures in various stages of healing.
- Staff refusing to allow or delaying visitors to see resident.
- Staff not allowing visitor to be alone with resident.
- Withdrawals, large or small, from bank accounts or change in financial business practices.
- Change in Last Will and Testament or other financial documents.[3]

Privately, pull back the sheet and look at their skin, extremities, hair and scalp, touch their hands and feet—are they cold, do you smell urine on them or in the room. The list is endless but you are their protector from being mistreated and poorly cared for. You

---

3 *http://www.nursing-home-abuse-resource.com.*

must continue to observe your family member's body and behavior. Be their eyes, ears and mouth. Speak out for them.

Below are definitions, examples, and signs and symptoms for each mistreatment category.

- **Physical:** Physical force that causes injuries, pain, or disabilities, including restraints.
  - » *Example:* Shaking, tightly holding, or hitting the older adult.
  - » *Signs and symptoms:* Broken bones, bruises, guarding, behavior changes.

  ▶ **Professional Case Example:** *A 93-year-old woman was brought to the Emergency Room (ER) by ambulance with a complaint of left hip pain. She was found lying on the floor at home in urine-soaked clothing by a home health aide. On arrival to the ER, she was not oriented to person, time and place, and responding, "I don't know" to multiple questions. The patient had bruising over the right eye and cheek. She also has bruising on shoulders and right upper thigh. The patient resided with her daughter and son-in-law who were in their 50s; the patient had been ambulatory and able to manage some activities of daily living (ADLs) prior to her arrival to the ER; and the son-in-law had expressed great anger over having his mother-in-law live with him and his wife and wished to have her live elsewhere. The patient's doctor visit two months prior to the ER visit was without any problems. The daughter was unable to explain the causes of her mother's bruises that were found upon examination at the ER.*

- **Emotional, psychological:** Verbal or nonverbal infliction of distress or emotional agitation, including isolation.
  - » *Example:* Using a loud tone of voice to say obscene words or use names other than the given names.
  - » *Signs and symptoms:* Agitation or withdrawal.

  ▶ **Professional Case Example:** *An 88-year-old widow with mild dementia lives with her daughter and five grandchildren (ages 2 to 11) in a three-bedroom apartment in a large city. Her daughter is recently widowed and moved in with her mother so that she may provide care for her. The daughter works two different jobs and a neighbor helps with care for the mother and children. The daughter brings her mother to the geriatric clinic because she is complaining of back pain and is becoming more confused. The mother has multiple bruises from tripping down the stairs. Her daughter states that her* *mother is "getting harder and harder to care for." The daughter also explains to the nurse that although her siblings would not assist her with caring for their mother, the siblings are unappreciative of her caregiving, constantly complaining and finding fault in the care provided, which usually leads to family fights and disagreements. The daughter further states that these disagreements make her feel anger toward her mother and her siblings.*

The nurse recommends counseling for the family and suggested that if the siblings do not go for counseling that the daughter needs to go so that she may learn how to manage her feelings about caring for her mother and how to deal with her siblings. Counseling was also recommended to assist with the stress of caring for five children and a mother and working multiple jobs.

- **Sexual:** Sex with older adults without their permission…even if they can't speak or communicate.
  - » *Example:* Rape.
  - » *Signs and symptoms:* Genital bruising or sexual infections, genital guarding.
- **Neglect or Abandonment:** Failure to meet agreed obligations to fulfill needs of the older adult or inappropriately leaving older person alone.
  - » *Example:* Lack provision for basic needs (food, shelter, clothes).
  - » *Signs and symptoms:* Malnutrition, dehydration, skin breakdown.
- **Financial or exploitive:** Inappropriate use of older adult's money or assets.
  - » *Example:* Caregiver cashes checks or spends money for personal gain.
  - » *Signs and symptoms:* Change banks, unable to pay bills, missing valuables.

ABUSE IN ANY KIND OF SKILLED NURSING FACILITY may not be as apparent until there are major physical or emotional problems. According to Nursing Home Abuse Resource, 30 percent of the nursing facilities in the United States are cited for abuse. And more alarming is the fact that the majority of abuse instances are never reported. The nursing home abuse statistics include severe instances of abuse ranging from death, to malnutrition and dehydration, inadequate medical care, and many other serious injuries and conditions. They suggest that if you or someone you love has been the victim of nursing home abuse, you should contact a nursing home abuse lawyer to learn your legal rights.

When Medicare and Medicaid were authorized by Congress in 1965, the Health Care Finance Administration of the United Sates Department of Health and Human Services was charged with enforcing nursing home regulations. While Congress authorized the first set of standards and continues to update the regulations, if the loved one's family caregiver does not report incidences, nothing will be done and thus the regulation will not be enforced. In most cases, when you mention observing a physical or emotional concern to an administrative staff person, they will deal with it right away.

> If your concern is not addressed with results, report it to the state agency that regulates nursing homes and assisted living facilities. Abuse of any type is unacceptable. Abusing those who are unable to speak up and protect themselves like children and the elderly is deplorable.

The media's coverage of elderly abuse cases indicates it could happen to your loved one. We encourage you to be mindful of this behavior whether it is physical, emotional, sexual, neglect, or financial—in the home or other type of housing facility. The first sign or knowledge of mistreatment of your loved one by you or a hired caregiver must be taken seriously and questions asked of the abuser and the abused. Handling these situations expeditiously will avoid future abuse encounters.

Journal

Caregiver and Loved One Abuse

- **How does my loved one respond verbally and emotionally to me, or their caregiver?**

_____

_____

_____

- **How does the caregiver respond verbally and emotionally to my loved one?**

_____

_____

_____

- **How many times have I noticed them responding differently to each other?**

_____

_____

- *Do I sense a concern about abuse from the caregiver?*

_____

_____

_____

_____

- *What options do I have to do something about it?*

_____

_____

_____

_____

_____

_____

_____

Additional Notes:

Chapter Fifteen

Taking Care of Yourself

Above all else, guard your heart, for it is the wellspring of life.
— Proverbs 4:23

CAREGIVERS MUST TAKE care of themselves while caring for others. According to the Family Caregiver Alliance, caregivers often experience increased blood pressure and insulin levels that may cause an impaired immune system, and they may be at higher risk for cardiovascular disease. A study of elderly spousal caregivers (ages 66 to 96) found that caregivers who experience caregiving-related stress have a 63% higher mortality rate than non-caregivers of the same age.[1]

Avoid these statistics—take good care of yourself. You cannot take care of someone else if you are also ailing.

When things get out of hand emotionally, call your health insurance provider's behavioral health division to explain the situation to their staff. The 1-800 number is

---

1 Family Caregiver Alliance, National Center on Caregiving. *www.caregiver.org.*

usually on the back of your health insurance plan card. Tell them you are having a family crisis. They will ask several standard questions, which the law requires them to ask. Afterwards they will discuss your present personal situation. Do not fear or feel alone—you are among the many people who rely on them for assistance every day. They will approve a certain number of sessions with the professional they determine you need and then supply you with the name and contact information. If, after the first appointment, you find you do not relate well with that professional, call back and they will offer another name and more information. The sooner you get help, the sooner you will return to feeling like yourself by having a clearer mind to live your life and handle your caregiving responsibilities with ease and compassion.

Additionally, your employer may also have an Employee Assistance Program (EAP) that can offer you help. EAP programs help employees to handle personal problems that might affect their work performance, health and well-being. They are usually associated with a health insurance plan or are offered as a no-cost benefit. The programs may vary but it's important to discover what services are available to you.

> *❧ **Personal Experience:** One time I recognized the need for more self-care when my mother was diagnosed with multiple myeloma a month after the death of my oldest aunt. Mother decided to get chemotherapy treatment for her cancer. Each month I would take her for her treatments, and while I was okay with seeing her and others receive therapy, it affected me. One day as I watched patients come in hairless, feeble but hopeful, my thoughts reflected on what could be the outcome for my mother later and possibly even myself at some time. I walked out and made a telephone call to my health insurance provider and said, "I have a family crisis. Is there anyone there that can help me?" I was given the 1-800 number for help.*
>
> *I was assigned a counselor who was very helpful in having me recognize what I was experiencing. The more I talked with her the better I felt. I began to understand what was happening emotionally and physically to my mother, my family, and myself. I faced this 'tension tiger' with the counselor and it went away like a 'tranquil tiger,' allowing me to perform my duties as family caregiver with love and patience.*

Continue to stay healthy by seeing your medical doctor, exercising daily, getting rest, eating healthy food, and drinking plenty of water. As odd as this may sound to those without diabetes, eliminate refined sugar and diet sodas from your diet.

❧ *Personal Experience: Another time I realized the need for me to take better care of myself happened when my mother and I were the healthcare advocates for my oldest aunt. The situation became so complex medically and administratively that I developed shingles. Shingles is a painful inflammation of the nerve fibers. The discomfort was one I'd wish to never have again or want anyone else to have.*

My doctor recommended I seek ways to manage the stress in my life. I started relaxing every morning in a warm tub of water with Epsom salt and lavender oil. This became my 'me time.' I could lie back in this soothing water as long as I had time because it was the beginning of my day. Even today, I continue to do this each morning when time allows.

ONE POWERFUL WAY to maintain your health is to develop a cadre of practitioners for services in addition to daily exercise. Some appropriate specialists include:

- Massage therapists
- Acupuncturists
- Nutritionists
- Chiropractors
- Meditation instructors
- Life coaches
- Fitness coaches and yoga instructors

❧ *Personal Experience: My next awakening to recognizing the need for more self-care came when I was at a doctor's appointment. My doctor asked me what was happening since my last appointment. I proceeded to tell her. She said, "slow down and take a breath." I was unaware of talking and not breathing. She explained, "I want to know what is going on but I also want you to use your breath to save your energy." She suggested I get massages to relax. I receive my first massage the next week and now they are a part of my personal survival protocol. When I don't have time or money for a full massage, a chair massage works just as well.*

Do not assume you cannot afford these practitioners. Look for schools teaching alternative health protocols in your area and make an appointment. You'll find reduced rates as compared with professional offices.

Tip: Ask for their most experienced student. The cost often proves quite reasonable.

ANOTHER PRACTICE I find extremely helpful in maintaining my emotional wellness is journaling. Each day, I write once, twice, or as many times as I feel the need—to express my positive and negative emotions. It allows me to let go of the things that don't serve me well and reinforce the positive with gratitude. Look for positives, and the positives will continue. Gradually the negatives go away, and the positives return again and again.

Following is a brief discussion of other stress management techniques.

Counseling

IF YOU BEGIN to feel overwhelmed and too busy to take care of yourself, or if your initial enthusiasm for being a caregiver begins to wane, don't beat up on yourself. Most family caregivers go through this dilemma at some point. It is important, however, that you reach out for help before your caregiving chores affect your health. As stated earlier, most health insurance cards have a toll-free number for inquiries on the back. If you have health insurance, call this number and ask if your plan covers professional counseling. Explain to the customer service representative answering your call that you are having a "family crisis" and need to find a counselor to help you. The representative may ask you routine questions to assess your needs and to determine the number of appointments you are allowed. Once you find a counselor, remember that if, after a first appointment, you don't feel comfortable with or can't relate to him or her, you can call the toll-free number again to request a different counselor.

A friend or family member can stay with your loved one while you go to the counseling appointment. Many people are willing to help you if you ask them in a timely manner.

Deep-Breathing Technique

LAY ON YOUR back with the palm of your left hand over your navel. Rest your right hand over your left hand. Keep your eyes open.

Imagine a balloon lying inside your stomach beneath your hands. Begin to inhale through your nose, imagining as you breathe that air is filling the balloon in your stomach. Continue to breathe and imagine the balloon is constantly filling up. Notice your rib cage and stomach expanding. Inhale for at least three seconds when you start this deep-breathing practice. Over time, increase the length of your inhalations to five seconds.

Slowly begin to exhale, completely emptying the balloon. As you do this, repeat to yourself the word "relax."

Exercise

YOU MAY FEEL that being on your feet all day and doing tasks for your relative is enough exercise. But you need to engage in physical activity that targets the areas of the body that require continual maintenance for good health—cardiovascular and muscular-skeletal systems. Try to carve a minimum of 15 minutes out of your schedule three times per week to exercise, working your way up to 30 and then 60 minutes a session. Go for a relaxing walk, ride a bicycle, or enroll in an exercise class. When you do something for others, you feel good. But when you do something for yourself, you feel replenished—which may give you the stamina to do even more for others.

Regular exercise enhances your health and self-esteem. It also:
- Distracts you from bothersome activities.
- Helps to increase the production of endorphins—the brain's feel-good neurotransmitters.
- Increases your self-confidence and reduces anxiety and depression.

Check local community fitness centers or the YWCA or YMCA for exercise classes. Go walking in a safe community or at a mall. Buy or borrow an exercise DVD from the library or search for an exercise class on cable TV. Remember to consult your doctor before starting any exercise program. Start slowly, and then gradually increase your level of exertion based on how you feel. Good luck!

Massage

MASSAGE IS A drug-free, non-invasive, humanistic approach to the body's ability to heal itself. A massage therapist uses his or her hands, fingers, forearms, and elbows to rub, press, and manipulate your skin, muscles, tendons and ligaments for relaxation and possible health benefits.

There are many types of massages, including:
- Deep-tissue
- Swedish
- Sports
- Trigger-point

Massages are known to:
- Relieve stress
- Relieve stiffness
- Boost the immune system
- Control blood pressure
- Alleviate pain
- Help manage anxiety and depression

Remember that massages can help you manage your stress, but they are not a substitute for medical care.

Proper Nutrition

WHENEVER WE CONSUME food, we are giving fuel to our bodies. Ideally, the fuel we put into our bodies is providing us with the proper nutrients. A doctor or dietician can help you tailor a diet to your needs by considering your health, lifestyle and food preferences.

When food shopping, stock up on fresh and unprocessed foods, including fruits and vegetables, whole-grain products and non-fat dairy products. It helps to avoid shopping for food when you are hungry.

Remember, the environment in which you eat plays a role in the nutritional value you get from a meal. When possible, eat with others, sit down when you eat and don't rush through a meal. Rushing may cause you to compromise chewing properly and result in poor digestion. A saying I remember from my youth goes: "Don't give your stomach what your teeth should have done."

Support Group

A SUPPORT GROUP can be a safe haven for a family caregiver to share good and not-so-pleasant experiences with people going through a similar experience. During these sessions—usually run by a group leader with professional experience—you may discover solutions and helpful tips from other caregivers who in turn may learn from you. It may take time for you to feel comfortable sharing personal information with strangers, but hang in there. Over time, the group may become a valuable source of support.

Ask your counselor or physician to recommend a support group for family caregivers. Some groups are free; others may have a nominal fee.

Yoga

THE PRACTICE OF yoga is an exceptional way to relieve stress. If you are new to yoga, try a beginner's class—its pace will be slower. Once you become familiar with the poses, you can practice them alone at home. You can also tailor your practice to fit your needs.

Before attending a class, tell your yoga instructor about medical conditions you may have. Ask what you should wear. Comfort and safety are essential for a successful experience. Starting with a beginner's class will help you avoid injuries. You may reach a point where you're ready to try more difficult poses. That's the time to move up to a more advanced class. But if doing yoga is a struggle for you, take at least three consecutive classes before you decide to quit. If you can't relate to your instructor, try a class with a different one.

Journal
Taking Care of Yourself

- ***What did I do for myself today?***

_____

_____

_____

- ***Which one of these services interests me?***

_____

_____

_____

- ***What is the contact information for the service?***

_____

_____

_____

_____

• *Additional notes:*

_____

_____

_____

_____

_____

_____

_____

_____

_____

_____

_____

_____

_____

_____

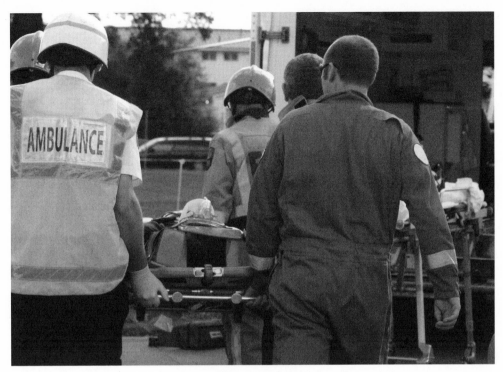

Chapter Sixteen

Medical Services

Behold, I will bring it health and healing:
I will heal them and reveal to them the abundance of peace and truth.
— Jeremiah 33:6

Curative Medical Services

CURATIVE CARE IS the treatment of your loved one to cure them of a disease or illness. It continues until the patient gets better and symptoms aren't present. Sharing with the doctors what you are told and what you observe is important. Symptoms such as weakness, fatigue, sleeplessness, irritability, loss of appetite, depression, and pain are a few of the physical and mental features of diseases to be shared with their doctor. This information is critical for the doctor to know in order to determine how to manage the care needed for your family member.

Family caregivers play a vital role in curative care of a loved one. They are considered partners with the healthcare team in keeping a loved one well. Being well is congruent with wellness, which has four parts: self-responsibility, nutritional awareness, physical activity, and management of stress.[1]

Self-responsibility maintains that the loved one has some degree of responsibility for their wellness. Be aware that some family members hold family caregivers responsible for their wellness. It is, therefore, incumbent upon the family caregiver to assist the loved one with owning at least some part of maintaining their wellness. A way to do this is to recognize things that the loved one enjoys about their wellness and hold them responsible for that portion. In addition, the family caregiver may add responsibilities for the loved one as they are able to handle them. For example, the loved one may have a negative attitude about eating because of nausea that accompanies chemotherapy. The family caregiver, in this instance, may empower the loved one with information as to how nutrition enhances the curative efforts of the healthcare team. Then the family caregiver would support and encourage the loved one for their involvement, regardless of how small. This in turn will motivate the family member to take charge of their own nutrition and hopefully change the negative thoughts of eating.

Nutritional awareness embraces learning about foods that keep the body physically and emotionally healthy. The healthcare team may provide this information via nutritional brochures and even classes that are offered. Appropriate caloric and nutritional intake is vital in assisting curative treatments because together these may strengthen the care recipient's body, including the immune system. Remember the phrase "We are what we eat." Therefore, if our food consumption is sufficient in amounts and nutritional values, we will maintain a sense of wellness.

Physical activity contributes to wellness through maintaining and improving body functions. The healthcare team must be consulted before beginning any form of physical activity. Physical activity may range from passive exercises (those performed by the caregiver) to aerobic exercises performed by the loved one. However, the healthcare team must approve any level. Physical activity releases endorphins and increases strength, flexibility, and balance. These are beneficial in keeping well and have been used to prevent falling.

Management of stress is important in maintaining wellness. Stress is the perception of displeasure and pleasure of events in daily life. Hormones are released during stressful events, which lead to biochemical changes in the body. If stress is sustained, these changes may lead to illness. Stress may be expressed by body movements, sweaty palms,

1 Touhy, T. (2008). Health and Wellness. In C. Jackson & A. S. Politte (eds.). *Toward Healthy Aging: Human Needs and Nursing Responses (7th ed.)*, St. Louis, MO: Mosby Elsevier.

irritability, inability to sleep, and increased heart rate. Loved ones and family caregivers may have stress. It is important to reduce stress when recognized. Methods of stress reduction include relaxation, exercise, yoga, deep breathing, and prayer and meditation.

IN SUMMARY, the healthcare team, the family caregiver, and the loved one work together toward curative care. All are needed to reach the highest potential for curative treatments. Therefore, it is an expectation for the family member and the family caregiver to interact with the healthcare team to achieve the best outcome of curative care.

> ▶ ***Professional Case Example:*** *A 65-year-old male was diagnosed with lung cancer. He had to endure radiation therapy prior to two rounds of chemotherapy and surgery. He was provided smoking cessation, dietary, and exercise instructions prior to surgery. He gradually improved his dietary intake and exercise until congruent with the healthcare team's recommendation and stopped smoking immediately. During the first round of chemotherapy he became weakened, and subsequently his wife assumed some of his activities of daily living such as making doctor appointments and running errands outside of the home. However, his attitude about eating decreased but he continued to eat as he acknowledged that this was necessary to maintain his nutritional values so that he could endure the chemotherapy. Although he could not continue to exercise at the same level now, he stretched is arms and legs via flexions and extensions and performed deep breathing exercises daily. After his surgery and second round of chemotherapy, his recovery time was reduced. When he was able, he resumed the diet and exercise recommended by the healthcare team.*

Interacting with Medical Services

THERE ARE TIMES when the family caregiver has to interact with medical services or the healthcare team, including calling 911 to get a loved one to the emergency room. The patient, family caregiver, and the healthcare team must work together to bridge gaps in knowledge deficits so that the best care is provided. The medical diagnosis and treatment for a disease or illness must come from your family member's doctor.

According to a critical care nurse at a Maryland hospital's Cardiac Surgery Intensive Care Unit, the family advocate is extremely important in the recovery and management of the ailing family member's care. She indicates, "The hospital medical team does what is necessary in the medical treatment, but it is the advocate and family that know the patient—when they are in a nonverbal state, happy, sad, or in pain. It is the advocate's responsibility to let a member of the medical team know whether what the team is doing is or is not working for their ailing family member. The role of the family caregiver is to provide emotional support and plead publicly on the loved one's behalf."

Family caregivers should use these comments as inspiration for doing the very best to interact with medical services throughout your ailing or elderly family member's healthcare experiences. Table 1 depicts characteristics that enhance interacting with the healthcare team and building relationships.

	Characteristics
Caregiver and Loved One	• Initiate / establish relationships • Be approachable • Be flexible • Advocate • Communicate needs • Ask pertinent questions
Healthcare Team	• Establish rapport / build trust • Be approachable • Be flexible • Advocate • Be proactive in meeting needs • Ask pertinent questions • Be sensitive to patient and family needs • Provide sensitive listening / effective communication

Table 1: Interacting with Medical Services—Characteristics

Personal Experience: Accompanying my mother to the emergency room many times allowed me to establish a procedure for future visits. I was awakened in the middle of the night many times with a call that went like this: "I hate to bother you but I'm in pain and feel very bad." You know your loved one is in distress by the tone in their voice so you say "I'll be right there." When

I got there and assessed the situation, I knew immediately to call 911.

After answering their questions and giving them the necessary information, I made her comfortable as possible. I learned to gather all her medications, driver's license for picture identification, and medical insurance cards to take with us. I never forgot after the first visit to take a warm jacket or sweater and snacks for sitting hours in the frigid ER area. This was my routine for all ER visits and going to doctor appointments. If you aren't prepared, you possibly will panic and cause the loved one to become alarmed.

▶ ***Professional Case Example:*** *A 60 year-old drove her 86 year-old mother with dementia secondary to Alzheimer's disease to the emergency room because the mother fell at home. The daughter, the primary caregiver, reluctantly answered questions to provide medical information about the patient to the healthcare team, and therefore, neglected to offer other essential information, which slowed down the history portion of the patient assessment.*

When the second healthcare provider approached the daughter, the daughter stated that she did not want to give information to the first provider because it seemed as though he was "short" with her and was not listening to what was said. The provider stated that there was no reason for the first provider's disposition, but informed the daughter of extenuating circumstances in the emergency room at the time and went on to say that the daughter had her undivided attention. This built rapport and trust with the daughter and therefore communication was optimal and needed care was provided. The daughter, then, felt free to answer and ask needed questions.

Although the first provider was "short" and not listening, the daughter (caregiver) should have informed the provider of her feelings and insisted (not being pushy, but being polite) so that the needs of the patient may be met expeditiously. Also, information and follow-through is missed when those involved do not assert themselves, which may increase the cost of care unnecessarily. The healthcare team is the caregiver's helper and if these two groups work together, there is nothing that cannot be accomplished or any need that cannot be met.

WHEN YOU CALL 911, the initial questions the operator will ask you are:

- ***What is your emergency?***
- ***What is your location?***

- *Questions regarding the sick person.*

Within a few minutes, the Fire Department or Emergency Medical Technician (EMT) will arrive. Make sure there is a house number visible from the street. If not, send someone out to flag down the ambulance. Keep pets and children out of the way to insure quick access to the sick or injured person.

The emergency service staff will check the person's vital signs and talk with them to assess their cognitive capability.

Important note: Let the patient answer questions if they are able, even if you know the answers.

Another staff member will request their picture ID, Medicare medical insurance card, and all medications your loved one is using.

Take along snack foods and water as you prepare to accompany your loved one for what might be a period of several hours before an outcome is decided by the medical team. Wear warm clothes—emergency rooms are kept cold in order to control the spread of germs. You may be allowed to ride in the ambulance; if not, you should meet them at the hospital.

The only time you should use an ambulance is when transporting a loved one to the hospital for an emergency, or, if necessary, for vital signs to be monitored during transport. The cost for round-trip transport is expensive unless you have insurance coverage for that service. Some communities offer memberships for their emergency transport systems. Be sure to know what is offered locally. Consult your telephone directory ahead of time for other sources for round-trip transportation of a bedridden or handicapped person to a doctor's appointment. It's helpful to have a telephone number list beside the telephone for easy access.

Let the doctor's office know that the patient will be arriving on a stretcher via special transport. They will tell you the best time to bring them and explain what the best access is to the office. Remember to take all current medications with you to the appointment.

Personal Experience: My oldest aunt had multiple strokes and was bedridden so the doctor appointments required an ambulance because she needed to be on stretcher. Because she couldn't sit for a long time the doctor's staff recommended bringing her in the side entrance to the office. This provides easier access for stretchers directly to patient treatment rooms thus bypassing the waiting area. The doctor sees her right away and she can return home.

The person going with her should take all medications to each doctor appointment to be reviewed. Remembering names of medications and dosages isn't necessary because they are conveniently indicated on the medication containers.

CREATE A FILE FOLDER for hospital visits and doctors' appointments. To make life less complicated, keep records of medical visits accessible.

Referring back to these records will happen more often than you might imagine. A habit that kept me abreast of medical information regarding my loved ones was my creation of a daily medical journal or log. I used a small spiral note pad that fit in my purse. As I talked and met with medical professionals, I would enter the date, the person's name and position or specialty, and results of the discussion. This was a very effective way for me to keep on top of what was a great deal of vital information.

❧ *Personal Experience: This was an important and necessary task with my younger aunt because she stayed in the hospital for a long time and couldn't communicate. As her healthcare proxy, I made decisions for doctors to perform tests and treatments on her. Every day I visited her there were many discussions with doctors and nurses. I found it easier to keep notes each time on who, when, what was discussed, and what was to be done by keeping a diary.*

My aunt was in a teaching hospital so there was always a team of medical students discussing her condition and recommending different tests and procedures. This allowed medical students to learn from what was done on a patient. On one occasion I didn't feel comfortable with this. I kept a record of each procedure and its results, and one day a request was made for a procedure to determine possible further treatment. I asked, "What does 'possible' treatment mean?" I told them I would think about it and let them know.

After reading my notes, I contacted my aunt's primary care doctor who knew her medical condition and asked for her opinion. On my next discussion with the hospital doctors, I asked, "If you go in and find she can't recover and live a better life, why do it?" They told me, "This is a teaching hospital and students learn from all we do." The risk outweighed the benefits so I declined the permission, and the lead doctor walked away very annoyed with my answer and me.

If I hadn't referred backed to my notes to recall the earlier discussions, I could have endangered my aunt's life. So keep a little spiral notebook to write all information about discussions with anyone pertaining your loved one's care or business. You do forget a lot and often during the family caregiver journey.

YOU WILL ENCOUNTER many challenges if your family member is admitted to a hospital. To minimize these difficulties, some hospitals are proactive in addressing quality medical support care for patients and their families. There is usually a department whose primary goal is visiting patients and asking questions to ensure the hospital staff is meeting the hospital's quality standard. If you have a concern and want to talk with this patient service representative ask the information desk for their telephone extension.

One Maryland hospital is striving, through their Patient/Family and Visitor Services Department, to make its patient, family, and visitor experience as comfortable and pleasant as possible. They describe their job as, "assisting to raise the hospital's quality standards to *superior* and *outstanding* instead of settling for *good.*"

This type of medical support service at a hospital is encouraging and helpful to all family caregivers who spend an exceptional amount of time throughout their journey helping others navigate medical facilities when there is a medical life-changing experience.

Tips: Visiting the Doctor
- Have a record of family medical history.
- Keep a record of surgeries and their dates.
- Take current medications with you. (The "Brown Bag" approach…place medications in a brown bag.)
- Make a list of supplements and vitamins your loved one takes.
- Make a list of questions to ask the doctor. There are no stupid questions, but it is stupid not to ask if you don't know.
- Ask the physician for permission to record the appointment.
- Ask loved one if they have any questions to ask the doctor.
- Tell the doctor of side effects of medication and allergies.
- Remember nurse's name.

DOCTOR VISITS MAY BE LESS CHALLENGING than going to a hospital because the physician's office is smaller and more personal. However, you can keep the frustration level down and the situation under control by staying organized.

I kept files labeled and alphabetized for three family members. The lesson is to do things immediately if it is your task to handle. If you have not heard from the other party, call to inquire about the status of the situation discussed on such a date. No one intends to forget important things, but we can get so busy that reprioritizing is constantly taking place. Don't allow this to happen at the expense of your loved one or your own life.

A great source for aids and supplies to help you address your medical situation is your local medical supply store. They offer many items and catalogs that will give you ideas on providing more efficient care for your loved one. A few examples:

- Protected covered spoons for feeding those with sensitive lips and teeth
- Hearing devices that amply sound for the individual when communication is needed
- Bed padding to protect beds from getting soiled
- Mechanical "grabbers" allowing greater reach for persons with restricted movement
- Jar openers, big-handled can openers, and many other gadgets for kitchen and bathroom that can ease your loved one's daily tasks in remarkable ways
- Lounge chairs that lift the seat to facilitate standing
- Urinals for your loved one who can't get to the bathroom

> *❧ **Personal Experience:** A circumstance for me needing extra help with medical supplies occurred with my oldest aunt. The latest strokes disabled her hands so she could not feed herself. She had to be fed by someone. The hands-on caregiver asks me to get a plastic-coated spoon. I went to the medical supply store and told them my situation, and they recommended the correct spoon for someone with sensitive lips and teeth. Their speediness in addressing my needs and knowledge of equipment caused me to contact them repeatedly for help with my special medical needs for my aunt and later for my mother.*

IF YOUR LOVED ONE is mobile, take them with you on your visit to the medical supply store. They can help you and the store's employees find the right items needed. The staff will suggest options for certain situations that you may never have considered would be helpful to you.

Ask the doctor or health insurance provider whether you can be reimbursed for these expenses and how to submit them for reimbursement. Don't assume you can't recoup these expenditures—just ask.

> *Tip:* Keep records and receipts for tax purposes listed under medical deductions.

One method for managing medical information is to acquire and organize medication lists, test and blood work results, and doctor reports. You can obtain these from the family physician who coordinates the health care with other specialists. By law, your loved one's medical information can be given to you but only if you hold a Durable Power of Attorney for healthcare. Some specialists will send the information to the family physician, so check with them to determine if they have received reports. This is your only way of ensuring that the family physician is aware of the total healthcare picture of your loved one. Remember to request this information at the appointment, and if you need to make a formal request for release of medical records you can do that before leaving the office as well.

If the family member is being cared for in the home, it is easier to observe daily changes. Reviewing this medical information prepares you to more effectively address any changes or observations with the physician. For example, blood work results indicate glucose reading, and if there is an increase or decrease, with or without apparent cause, the doctor will determine how to address the situation. He or she will notice such changes in results but as the advocate for your loved one it is essential that you be aware of any medical changes as well.

> *Personal Experience:* I remember an occasion during my mother's illness when her hired caregiver called me and said, "I'm concerned. Your mother is not like herself. She doesn't want to eat, but is just sleeping. I'm concerned." I went to her apartment to check on her. I asked Mom several questions to determine her mental alertness. She understood what I was asking me and answered me. I e-mailed the oncology nurse and described Mother's situation. The nurse reminded me of Mother's just receiving that week the first chemotherapy treatment with a new drug. Mother was experiencing side effects from the treatment. This didn't make my mother or us feel better but explained what she was experiencing. I was to e-mail again if that continued or got worse. Of course, the side effect subsided and I didn't have to contact her.
>
> Another occasion of noticing medical changes was when my aunt was

living in a rehabilitation center. When I walked in her room, she was asleep. I pull up a chair and sat by her bed to hold her active hand. She eventually opened her eyes and they weren't their usual brightness but had a glazed over appearance. She didn't acknowledge me in any way. This was different so I went to the nurses' station to inquire about her status. I asked her nurse how she was doing and was there a reason for her being drowsy. She tells me, "Your aunt went for a treatment and we gave her Percocet for pain." I was relieved and happy I asked because my aunt seemed close to death to me. The next day she was quite different.

My advice to you is to ask when you see or are told that your loved one experienced a medical or emotional change.

INTERACTING WITH MEDICAL SERVICES in a skilled nursing facility is different than caring for loved ones in a private home. The family caregiver should request these reports from the staff periodically.

- *Medication list*
- *Laboratory results*
- *Doctors' orders*
- *Physical and occupational therapists' orders*

Find out what the facility's policy is for obtaining medical records. Reviewing this information will keep you informed to address concerns as needed.

If you are taking a family member to a physician consultation appointment, remember to take these records with you. Remind medical and skilled nursing staff of the facility of your family member's appointment a few days ahead of time. They will prepare the appropriate medical records for you to take with you. Remember when the consulting physician diagnoses and makes a medical request of the facility, you must have a doctor's order or prescription to present to the facility before the orders can be carried out. These can be hand carried back to the facility or be faxed from the doctor's office before you leave. This includes a doctor's order for types of meals needed. For example, my mother became anemic from her chemotherapy, and it was important that all of her meals were filled with nutrients. Once the doctor's orders were faxed, the skilled nursing facility could make the necessary change to her diet. *Your word is not enough for care of this kind to be changed—they must have the doctor's order.*

➳ *Personal Experience: I experienced this situation when my mother lived in the skilled nursing area of her retirement community and I accompanied her to an office visit with her oncologist. Waiting to see the doctor was a time to catch up on things she needed to tell me. She said, "Dinner last night was okay, but I just can't get them to bring me a salad with only iceberg lettuce." I knew she had mentioned it to them, and I also had said something to dietary but didn't know personal verbal request were acknowledged courteously but nothing was done. Request for staff were only done through a medical order from a doctor.*

Mother was on a blood thinner, Coumadin, so she couldn't eat leafy vegetables. The oncologist wrote the dietary order for iceberg lettuce in her salad at this appointment.

You and your loved one must remember to request a doctor's order for whatever is needed when they live in a medical facility.

Journal
Medical Services

- **What is the best way for me to keep a record of medical information?**

_____

_____

_____

_____

_____

_____

- **What changes in my loved one should I report to the doctor or medical team?**

_____

_____

_____

_____

_____

- ***Additional notes:***

Chapter Seventeen

Diseases and Conditions

As to disease, make a habit of two things—to help, or at least, to do no harm.
— Hippocrates

Stroke Information

DURING MY THREE experiences as a caregiver, my three loved ones had different major diseases—stroke and cancer. Recovery and treatment was difficult because of the patients' ages. My recommendation to everyone is to do research immediately after the doctor gives you the diagnosis of a loved one's condition so you will know what questions to ask.

There are many resources available to understand the definition, causes, treatment and rehabilitation of the disease. According to the Hartford Hospital Stroke Center[1], a stroke is a brain injury that occurs when the blood supply is interrupted, thus causing a sudden loss of function.

1 Stroke Center. *Learn About Conditions and Procedures*, Hartford, Connecticut.

One or more of the following can cause blood flow interruption:

- ***Damage to blood vessels supplying blood to the brain.***
- ***An injury or clot that forms and breaks off from another part of the body.***
- ***Local blood clots (plaque) forming along the inner lining of the arteries.***
- ***Inflammatory conditions in the blood vessels.***

There are two major types of strokes. A ***hemorrhagic stroke*** occurs when the blood vessel breaks and bleeds into or around the brain. An ***ischemic stroke*** is caused when a clot stops blood supply to an area of the brain. Immediate treatment is needed to dissolve a clot causing an ischemic stroke and to stop the bleeding during a hemorrhagic stroke. Other treatment will attempt to reduce chances of other strokes, improve functioning, and overcoming disabilities. The rehabilitation process involves physical therapy to gain as much movement as possible, occupational therapy to assist in everyday tasks and self-care, and speech therapy to improve swallowing and relieve speech difficulties.

> ❧ ***Personal Experience:*** *Two aunts had strokes that affected their ability to care of themselves. One became progressively worse while the other aunt had extreme damage very shortly after her initial stroke. Both continued to have small strokes throughout the remainder of their lives. Their first strokes were life-changing experiences that put an end to the active lives they knew for many years.*
>
> *One aunt had a traumatic experience that led to a stroke and the other aunt wasn't even aware of the warning signs for the onset of strokes; therefore, care wasn't given soon enough to avoid extensive damage.*

Make sure you know the warning signs of strokes. Knowing these signs may keep your loved one or you from possible severe stroke damage. According to the American Heart Association, if you notice one or more of these signs, don't wait.[2] Call 911 or your emergency medical services. **You must get the patient to a hospital right away.**

Symptoms of Stroke

- Sudden numbness or weakness of the face, arm or leg, especially on one side of the body
- Sudden confusion, trouble speaking or understanding
- Sudden trouble seeing in one or both eyes
- Sudden trouble walking, dizziness, loss of balance or coordination
- Sudden, severe headache with no known cause

2 Source: American Heart Association, *Stroke Warning Signs*. 2010.

For additional information on strokes, do a Google search on strokes or ask your physician for more information. There are many hospitals and medical sites that give an in-depth explanation of strokes, their causes, and treatment options.

Cancer Care

Caring for a loved one who is suffering from cancer is often bittersweet. Initially, the patient is distraught and immediately thinks they are dying when cancer is discovered. While death is something we all must face someday, it tends to be more imminent with a cancer diagnosis than with other medical conditions. Yet many a cancer crisis can ultimately be life enriching.

You should be prepared for the first and subsequent oncologist visits if chemotherapy treatment is chosen. On the first appointment, it is essential to have someone accompany the patient. Usually they are very fearful and they hear only what they want to hear, missing the critical details. Make a list of questions so you will not lose track of what to ask the doctor. The doctor will appreciate your preparation and the good relationship begins.

Below is a list of suggested questions offered by the *cancer.org* website.[3]

- What kind of cancer do I have?
- At what stage is my cancer?
- Can this stage cancer be treated?
- What therapy are you suggesting and why?
- Will this therapy cure the cancer or just manage the symptoms?
- What are the dangers in this therapy?
- What are the side effects of the treatment?
- What are the symptoms associated with this therapy?
- What are the advantages and disadvantages of this treatment?
- Are there other therapies you would recommend? Why? or Why not?
- How often and when are these treatments given?
- How long will I have to have therapy?
- How will this alter my life at home, work, or spare time?
- What medicines are you suggesting, and what are their purpose?
- Is this the only drug I will be taking?
- Will we know if the drug is working?
- Why and how often do you need blood work?

---

3 *www.cancer.org.*

- Will someone coordinate the treatment procedure with other doctors?
- What problems and symptoms should be reported to you immediately?
- Is there a best time to call the office? When?
- Is the drug working or not working when I have no symptoms?
- How likely is it my cancer will reoccur with this therapy?
- How do I prepare for the treatment?
- Does this treatment harm my ability to have children?
- Are there any dietary restrictions, and what recommended foods should I eat before or after the therapy begins?
- May I drink alcohol during therapy?
- What will this therapy cost me?

EVENTUALLY, THE PATIENT realizes that worrying is not going to cure their cancer. Instead, the patient often starts to develop a positive outlook as friends encourage them and share their experiences or other friends' experiences. Another technique is to practice your faith continually. Things may begin to feel more hopeful and positive.

Doctor visits will stop feeling so dreadful. Prescribed therapy can begin to help in restoring cancerous cells to healthy ones. The patient must be reminded of the importance of both therapy and a positive outlook—only they can help themselves overcome this battle.

This is the bitter part, while you are encouraging the loved one, you will have to get over the shock of the diagnosis by yourself. It is essential to keep your best face on and maintain a positive attitude at all times. The sweet portion comes when your loved one accepts their diagnosis.

> *Personal Experience: The sweet turning point for me was going to the first appointment at the oncologist's office with my mother. While in the reception area, I observed others and overheard conversations between more seasoned patients. They were sharing their journey with this disease. Some were laughing at what they did and thought before their actual therapy began. But now they were bubbling with joy and hope. While my mother thought it was depressing, it was what I needed to hear to continue encouraging her. As we returned home, I asked her whether she had heard the people talking about their experiences. No, she had not. So, I shared with her their stories. She would say, "Really, that's great. Maybe that's what I will experience." And today she says, "Remember how I was when I first went to the cancer*

*center?" To hear her say this brings joy to my heart. This is sheer sweetness
to any cancer victim's family.*

THIS PART OF THE JOURNEY must be travelled alone; everyone gets through these stages in their own time—in their own way. You can only provide love, support, be gentle and take one day at a time—*Be in the moment.*

Caring for a cancer patient is complex. It is unpredictable because it doesn't follow a predictable course of development or treatment. However, diseases like strokes, diabetes, Alzheimer's, and coronary disease, once diagnosed, tend to follow a rather predictable course if the patient takes the prescribed medications and follows the doctor's orders. Cancer, on the other hand, is a chronic disease. It may go into remission—giving the patient a false sense of hope, and sometimes returning even when the patient follows the doctor's orders. I am not downplaying the seriousness of these other diseases, but cancer can take the patient and family on a relentless roller coaster ride.

> ❧ ***Personal Experience:*** *This was my mother's second cancer episode. When she was younger she had breast cancer and twenty years later she developed multiple myeloma—cancer of the red blood cells in the plasma of the bone marrow.*
>
> *The breast cancer was discovered early enough and she didn't receive chemotherapy treatment. Each year she had to have a mammogram done by a physician. In spite of these diseases, my mother lived a full life until age 93. She questioned her bill and wrote the last check for her residence fee at the retirement community skilled nursing area. She was mentally alert until the last few hours of her life.*

Dementia

Dementia is a syndrome that is characterized by symptoms that have varying causes and may be reversible or irreversible. Some reversible causes of dementia are hypothyroidism, depression, and drug toxicity that can be cured by treating the cause of the symptoms. Irreversible causes of dementia, including Alzheimer's disease, Parkinson's disease, and strokes, have no cure. The variation of these symptoms is large and is the reason dementia patients are not similar. Possible symptoms are:

- Memory loss—constantly forgetting
- Problem with speech—use of word and meaning
- Difficulty performing familiar tasks that previously were very easy

- Orientation in time and place—where am I? There is uncertainty about the date and year
- Personality problem—hard to handle
- Having doubts—going to see the doctor

Symptoms presented here are general and may also be found in any type of dementias. The National Stroke Association indicates some of the same risk factors for strokes are the same as for vascular dementia—high blood pressure, history of previous stroke, heart disease, and high cholesterol.[4] Common types of dementias include—Alzheimer's disease, Lewy Body dementia, vascular dementia, and Parkinson's disease.

According to Alex Mayor, a psychologist working in the psycho-geriatric department in a hospital, there are several possible symptoms displayed over time by dementia patients.

> ✤ *Personal Experience: My aunt with the immediate extreme damage of stroke developed vascular dementia, a loss of her cognitive function. She had a paralyzed left side of her body, and was bedridden. She could no longer chew or swallow solid food. Her speech was slow and slurred. Occasionally, she would shift from present to past times.*

Alzheimer's Disease

Alzheimer's disease is puzzling and feared by most people because they lack a detailed knowledge of its symptoms. It is responsible for 50-80 percent of dementias.[5]

According to the Alzheimer's Association, these are some of the symptoms:[6]

- Memory loss that disrupts daily life
- Challenges in planning or solving problems
- Difficulty completing familiar tasks at home, work or at leisure
- Confusion with time or place
- Trouble understanding visual images and spatial relationships
- Problems with words in speaking or writing
- Misplacing things and losing the ability to retrace steps
- Decreased or poor judgment
- Withdrawal from work or social activities
- Changes in mood and personality

4 National Stroke Association *Vascular Dementia and Strokes*, 2010. *http://www.stroke.org/site/PageServer?pagename=VADEM.*
5 Alzheimer's Association. *www.alz.org.*
6 Ibid.

They describe the difference between Alzheimer's and typical age-related changes in this manner:

Signs of Alzheimer's	Typical age-related changes
• Poor judgment and decision making	• Making a bad decision once in a while
• Inability to manage a budget	• Missing a monthly payment
• Losing track of the date or the season	• Forgetting which day it is and remembering later
• Difficulty having a conversation	• Sometimes forgetting which word to use
• Misplacing things and being unable to retrace steps to find them	• Losing things from time to time

Table 2: Alzheimer's and typical age-related changes.[7]

A FAMILY CAREGIVER and family member with a loved one who has Alzheimer's disease has a challenging emotional experience ahead. The symptoms observed may vary or be simultaneously combined with other features of the disease. ***Remember, this is the disease and not your loved one's purposeful behavior.***

The one thing each of the family caregivers admits is you reach the point of knowing you can't appropriately and safely care for your loved one with Alzheimer's disease. Eventually, you determine it is unsafe for them and those around them. The personal experiences below reflect some of the different situations and how their families dealt with it.

> *❧ **Personal Experience of a Friend:** We knew that my mom's memory had been slowly slipping for years but as long as she and Dad were together they could continue to function as an independent unit. With his sudden death it was painfully clear that she was a victim of Alzheimer's and was not capable of living on her own. As my siblings and I all held full time jobs it wasn't a realistic option to have her live with one of us. We felt very guilty looking for an assisted living facility for Mom but knew that this was the safest option for her.*
>
> *My sister and I each used local resources from the state, plus our companies EAP programs to quickly develop a list of nearby facilities that specialized in memory impairment. We selected one after a whirlwind of visits and for*

---

7 Ibid.

several years my mom was pretty stable and content with her situation. The facility was wonderful and the residents were very sociable. Meals were eaten together in the dining room and the residents spent a lot of time together. Unfortunately the disease is progressive and as time went on she forgot who we were (which was really hard to deal with) and slowly lost the ability to maintain any interest in social contact. This is a cruel disease as it slowly robs a person of all of the thoughts and memories that made them who they are. Toward the end it was more about making sure she was safe and well cared for as the disease slowly eroded her mental and physical capabilities.

I have heard it said that this is a disease that is often worse for the family than it is for the victim and I would certainly agree with that. You have to do the best you can at each stage to make sure you are providing a positive supportive and safe environment, and I am grateful that there are such good assisted living facilities available. Home care may be an option in some families but I think it would be very difficult to provide for all of the needs of the Alzheimer's patient 24/7. It took just over six years for the disease to run its course and my mom to pass on. We celebrate the smart, funny and extremely capable person she was for most of her life and try not to just mourn the Alzheimer's victim.

Personal Experience of a Friend: Alzheimer's is one of those rare conditions that eventually becomes easier for the patient to deal with as the disease progresses, and more difficult for the family members. I saw first-hand the effects of the disease, and the toll (both financial and emotional) it takes on the family.

The early stages of Alzheimer's are difficult for everyone. Before my grandmother was diagnosed with the disease, there were periods when she could focus her energy and appear to everyone that she was a normal, functional senior citizen. Then there were the days when you wondered where she was, and if she was going to return from the grocery store just around the corner. She eventually returned, with a new dent in the side of the car, complaining that she did not know what was wrong with the people who parked in that parking lot, since they were always leaving a new dent in her car.

As the disease progressed, the times she could pull it together and appear to have no issues became fewer and fewer. More often, the signs something was wrong were becoming the norm, and questions were raised about senile dementia, or even worse, the prospects of Alzheimer's. She became angry, with more of the anger focused on her, as she found it more difficult to carry on a conversation, as she could not remember words or basic facts. We had no idea how bad things had become until my grandfather passed away. It quickly became clear that he had been able to cover for her for some time and had been bearing the brunt of the disease for some time.

My grandmother quickly started to deteriorate after the death of my grandfather. My mother originally planned on taking care of my grandmother, but I pointed out that this was going to be a 24/7 job. How would she feel if she awoke to find that my grandmother had wandered off in the middle of the night? Did my mother know what kind of care was going to be needed? Could she meet the other healthcare issues that were going to occur as a result of the disease and her continual aging? It was clear that a nursing home was not only the best option—it was the only option.

I understand the guilt my mother faced at first. Here was the person who had raised and taken care of her. There is a sense of duty and responsibility that made her want to provide for my grandmother. As the disease progressed, the wisdom of the nursing home option became clear. There were more health issues that started; these required more care and special treatments than we could provide. My grandmother became more confused and less able to converse with us. Each of us encountered a point when she could not remember who we were. The time came where she stopped being able to recognize my mother, and would actually ask mother if she knew where her daughter was. To me, this was when my grandmother died. The vessel that she had resided in was being left behind.

My grandmother continued to "live" for almost three years. My mother was frustrated and we all wondered what the point was to this continued existence. The only salvation that I took from it was my grandmother couldn't have cared less at that point. She knew no difference, and since she was not in pain, one day was no better or worse than any other.

At the end, everyone felt that my grandmother had finally been granted a release from this world when she passed away. The general feeling was a sense of relief and that she had in fact passed away years before.

Journal
Diseases and Conditions

- **What diseases are in my family history?**

_____

_____

_____

- **Which relatives had these diseases?**

_____

_____

_____

- **What do I need to know about each of these diseases?**

_____

_____

_____

- **To whom and where can I go to get more information on the diseases in my family?**

_____

_____

_____

Chapter Eighteen

End-of-Life Services

God grant me the serenity to accept the things I cannot change,
the courage to change the things I can, and the wisdom to know the difference.
— Reinhold Niebuhr

THE EXPERIENCE WE never look forward to is the death of a loved one. Just as ending life is inevitable for all of us, grief for survivors is normal but always difficult. When a loved one has a terminal illness, they can receive palliative care and hospice care to help prepare them for dealing with death. The family can receive help in dealing with the grieving process. The comforting news is that both services are available through Medicare.

The Caregiver's Role

There are many roles that the primary family caregiver assumes during the end-of-life experience. These include:

- Caregiver
- Comforter
- Teacher
- Preacher
- Friend
- Family counselor
- Bearer of bad news, good news, and unwanted news

Those who mourn the loss of their loved one will need help with:

- Acknowledging the reality of death
- Embracing the pain of loss
- Changing the relationship with the person who died from presence to memory
- Developing a new self identity
- Searching for new meaning
- Receiving support from others (don't reject it as some mourners do, isolating themselves from others)

Palliative Care

What is palliative care? Palliative care is the protocol a medical team puts in place to keep a person comfortable and improve the patient's quality of life as they prepare to die. It is available for those with very serious chronic or terminal illnesses. The main purpose is to relieve symptoms, not to cure a disease or illness.

The palliative care team consists of doctors, nurses, social workers and other medical professionals. This care is most often received in a medical facility such as a hospital, skilled nursing home, or extended care facility.

The team provides the following kinds of care:

- Treatment of pain
- Help the patient understand healthcare procedures and policies
- Patient and family emotional and spiritual support
- Communication in a private but personal manner
- Help in understanding treatment options and choices
- Explaining information that is difficult to understand and/or difficult to accept

When the time comes to make the decision whether or not to have palliative care, the doctor is the best source of information. For example:

- What is the professional philosophy of the palliative care team being referred to you?
- How is the care paid for?
- Is there a time limit for the services?
- Are there any restrictions?
- Where do you receive treatment?

This discussion can occur with or without your loved one present, depending upon their medical and psychological status. If they are capable of making decisions and understanding what is being said, they can make the decision regarding palliative care themselves. Otherwise, the decision is the responsibility of the designated family member. Remember, there are no bad or good decisions, just difficult ones.

> **Personal Experience:** *All three of my loved ones for whom I was the primary caregiver received palliative care into their end-of-life stage. One aunt was the recipient of palliative care through her doctor at the hospital. After they determined there wasn't anything medically to cure or improve my oldest aunt's life, they spoke with me to make the decision to keep her comfortable.*
>
> *Family members were told her status and could come by to see her. Those who visited had private time with her to say what they wanted to say. After a few days, she was under constant watch by the hospital.*
>
> *The amazing part of this experience was the sense of peace that came in the room as the chaplain was in her room, and her hired caregiver and I stood at her bedside talking softly. I held her hand as I always did. This time, as I held it she released that last breath of life. Death gently came into her body and left her and us at peace.*

Hospice Care

Hospice and palliative care are similar. Palliative care can be offered without hospice services, but hospice care includes palliative services.

> **Personal Experience:** *My other aunt and my mother received palliative care through hospice service. This aunt received hospice services for a few days at the hospital after a talk with my cousin, a physician, who guided me through her last severe medical change. Because I lived out of town, he visited her and conferred with the hospitalist assigned to her. He explained the situation to me and a decision had to be made on what to do next. She was transferred back to the rehabilitation center where she lived. Upon her return she was reassigned to their hospice provider. It is always a tough decision, but you don't want your loved one to continue suffering and be in pain. You make the decision and ask for peace of mind from your Divine Creator.*
>
> *During the initial time of her illness, I was told by her doctor not to talk to her about the business she could no longer operate. He felt it would be too*

traumatic for her to hear about the closing of the business. However, I always felt she wanted to ask me but never could utter the words. Interestingly, the day before she died, I sat by her bed holding her hand as I always did. On this day I told her, "I have something I think you want to know." She listened as I told her that the family wanted her taken care of for the rest of her life and in order to do that the decision was made to close the business. This was done at the advice of the attorney's firm. She appeared to look at me with such relief in her eyes as if to say, thank you. I asked her if that was okay, and she moved her head up and down. Not only was this a relief for her but for me also. Early the next morning, I received a call that she peacefully ended her earthly journey.

Hospice Care

A hospice service provides a professional team approach to improve your loved one's quality of life and dignity by keeping them pain-free and symptom-free. It is a program for people in the last stages of incurable diseases. The team consists of doctors, nurses, social workers, counselors, home health aides, clergy, therapists, and trained volunteers. The loved one, doctor, and responsible family member decide when hospice care should begin. Medicare pays for this service when provided by a certified hospice program.

SITUATIONS OFTEN DELAY HOSPICE CARE because patient and family feel death is imminent. Some think hospice will cause their loved ones to lose hope and give up. Thoughts that focus on the final hospice stage—death—can overshadow the good features of hospice. Some people in hospice care have gone into remission and returned to palliative care, thus going out of hospice while enjoying life, family and being pain-free. When your loved one has these experiences, they may be suspended from hospice care by the hospice doctor or re-certified to return to hospice by the loved one's doctor.

Additional services are offered as part of hospice care that enhance the care that may be offered such as:

- *Spiritual Care:* Your loved one's spiritual needs are unique to them. Hospice will take into account their preferences when determining how to proceed.

- *Respite Care:* This allows family members to take a break from providing continuous daily care—a chance to get away briefly. However, each hospice program determines the amount of time so make sure you ask about it.

- **Family Conference:** The nurse and social worker will regularly discuss your loved one's condition and what to expect in the days ahead.
- **Bereavement Care:** Grieving after the loss of a loved one is difficult, so hospice may offer support to the survivors as well. The hospice team may stay in contact and can aid the family through support groups for up to a year after the death of their loved one.

Hospice has a special way of caring for your loved one and your family. They teach us how to live with loss.

For more information on palliative care, contact your physician. Or, ask your loved one's doctor to refer you to a hospice team for a consultation. The enrollment process includes an assessment by hospice nurses. You may also contact a national hospice organization such as the National Hospice and Palliative Care Organization, American Cancer Society, and the National Cancer Institute for further references.

> **Note:** Medicare will not cover both hospice and private doctor care at the same time. Once the loved one enters a certified hospice service, they are under the care of the hospice medical team who is reimbursed my Medicare. If the loved one improves to the point that they no longer need hospice they are suspended and their case reverts back to their private physician who can resume filing for the cost of coverage with Medicare.

► ***Professional Case Example:*** *An 85-year-old widow is recently moved to be close to her children because she recently lost her husband of 65 years. This widow was diagnosed with lung cancer three years ago and currently has been diagnosed with colon cancer. She weighs 80 pounds after losing 30 pounds over the past six months. She has consistent pain, has significantly decreased mobility, and needs assistance with bathing, dressing, and feeding. Therefore a home healthcare referral is made and weekly visits initiated. She tells the home health staff that she cared for her husband until he died and that her children know better than to place her anywhere other than home. She has a live-in sitter and her daughter visits weekly. The home health nurse encourages the widow to accept hospice with palliative care services and to establish a health care proxy (her son), which she accepts. Care is provided at the level desired by the widow.*

Upon the next visit, the home health nurse notices that the widow is visibly worse. The widow has called her children and other family members to say her good-byes for closure. Her children are arguing—stating the son with healthcare proxy wants more therapies for their mother and the daughter argues that her mother does not want heroic efforts and since this is what her mother wants this is what they should do for their mother.

There are times when healthcare proxies may make decisions against what the individual desired. It is vital that the care recipient talk candidly about their wishes before making the final proxy designation.

Complementary and Alternative Therapy (CAM)

To enhance the palliative and hospice care, consider other therapies that complement conventional medicine.

A combination of diverse medical and health care systems, practices, and products that are not presently considered part of conventional medicine in the United States (National Center for Complementary and Alternative Medicine, 2002). This is a form of palliative care that focuses on establishing functional independence and improving quality of life.

The following are examples of Complementary and Alternative Therapy:

- Herbal Medications
- Pet Therapy
- Music Therapy
- Meditation
- Tai Chi
- Aroma Therapy
- Massage Therapy
- Chiropractic Therapy
- Acupuncture
- Acupressure
- Water/Spa Therapy
- Water Aerobics
- Breathing Exercises
- Hypnosis

WHILE THESE THERAPIES have demonstrated great benefits for some, they do have risks. You should consult their physician before beginning any of these therapies.

The experience of "anticipatory grief" will appear again at this point of your journey. The symptoms wouldn't be different—just more intense because the time seems imminent once end of life services are discussed. Read the previous discussion about "anticipatory grief" on page 110 to recall what is normal for you to experience during this time. What you learned to do before when the symptoms appeared will help you to successfully get through this "anticipatory grief" episode easier.

Journal
Palliative Care

- ***My loved one is ready for death because he/she said:***

_____

_____

_____

_____

- ***My loved one is not ready for death because he/she said this happened today:***

_____

_____

_____

- ***My loved one is comfortable with palliative care because these are the changes I see:***

_____

_____

_____

- *I am pleased with my loved one's palliative care because I see these changes:*

_____

_____

_____

_____

- *What complementary and alternative therapies do I think will help my loved one?*

_____

_____

_____

_____

- *Additional notes:*

_____

_____

_____

_____

Journal

Hospice Care

- **My loved one was quick to accept hospice care because these things were said and/or happened.**

_____

_____

_____

- **My loved one likes these aspects of hospice care.**

_____

_____

_____

- **What do I like about hospice care?**

_____

_____

_____

- **What complementary and alternative therapies will help my loved one?**

_____

_____

_____

Journal
Anticipatory Grief

- ***As a family caregiver, what are my feelings towards palliative and hospice care?***

Palliative:

_____

_____

_____

_____

Hospice:

_____

_____

_____

_____

- ***What sad symptoms am I experiencing today?***

_____

_____

_____

_____

- *My concerns are:*

_____

_____

_____

_____

- *The techniques I used from my previous list are:*

_____

_____

_____

_____

- *The ones most effective were:*

_____

_____

_____

_____

- *Additional notes:*

_____

_____

_____

_____

_____

_____

_____

_____

_____

_____

_____

_____

_____

Chapter Nineteen

Approaching Death Tasks

Nothing quite brings out the zest for life in a person like the thought of others approaching death.
— Author Unknown

IF YOUR LOVED ONE has discussed with you and documented his or her wishes before death, carrying out the tasks of death will be easier. If you don't know your loved one's wishes, however, a religious leader or funeral director can make suggestions for different services.

There are several options for memorializing your loved one:
- **Traditional funeral and burial service**
- **Embalming, memorial service and burial service.**
- **Embalming and graveside service**
- **Cremation and memorial service**
- **Cremation only**

Exploring Funeral Service Options

FUNERAL AND CREMATION businesses price their services in different ways. A few of the pricing methods used are:

- Packages.
- Item by item.
- Prearranged planned agreements.

Narrow your search to about three funeral homes. You can also search online for cost of funerals, just to give you some idea of prices and services to be considered. Be prepared, when you meet the director, with a list of questions, or search online for a checklist. There are many websites that will provide you with this information.

These are some of the questions you should ask:

- ***What is the process for a burial or cremation services?***
- ***What is the cost of each alternative?***
- ***What budget do you need for a tasteful service?***
- ***May I have your pricelist? (By law, they should have one for you.)***

When they tell you it all depends on what you choose, ask whether they have any recommendations. Follow up by asking why for each recommendation. Remember that funeral homes are in business to make money. Keep in mind that your agenda is to be informed and to make a wise decision that meets your and your family's needs.

There may be non-profit organizations in your area that offer assistance with funeral planning. However, you may verify the pricing for services and merchandise of a for-profit business or non-profit group through the Federal Trade Commission's Consumer Protection Guide for Funerals. The Federal Trade Commission was established to prevent unfair method of businesses offering their services and products to the general public.

Prearranged Services

HOPEFULLY, YOUR LOVED one made arrangements for his or her funeral before getting ill. But if he or she didn't, you may have to take responsibility for this task—preferably before your loved one dies.

When prearranging services before the death of a loved one there are different options available:

- Discuss pre-funding funeral services with a funeral director.
- Contract services to match loved one's life insurance proceeds.
- Pay with cash after death has occurred.
- Purchase burial insurance that fully qualifies for recipients of Supplemental Security Income and Medicaid.

There are advantages to prearranging funeral services:
- Your loved one is more objective, and a financially realistic decision is possible.
- Price and selection of the most costly item, the casket, and other services are secured.
- With the Power of Attorney, you can make prearrangements without your loved one being present, allowing you to keep costs under control.
- You can make wiser, more thoughtful decisions because you're not yet grieving over a loss.
- You give yourself time to change your mind about the funeral services.

THERE ARE SOME PITFALLS to prearrangement that you should be aware of:
- Your loved one's prepaid choices are not up to the family's expectations and costly changes are made.
- The funeral company is out of business and another business will not honor the contract at the same cost.
- You paid for services in full only to learn that money was not held in a trust fund by the funeral home or its bank.

Service Cost Coverage

Payment of expenses may come from the following sources:
- Life insurance policy
- Prearranged services
- Family contributions
- Veterans Administration benefits
- State coverage—embalming and burial only

THIS SEEMS A LOT TO REMEMBER, but if you plan some of these tasks ahead of time, you will be less frustrated and not have to handle them in the midst of family and friends.

One additional consideration to planning a funeral is to know how to effectively handle the death of someone with a public persona. Handling the news media discreetly is critical along with having a recent photograph of the person for them to use. As sad as it may be, many individuals may try to use this opportunity to seek financial gain. Please beware of photographers, historians, marketing entities, and charities.

What to do with your loved one's historical items will be a big decision. I chose to donate my loved one's artifacts to the city public library, because I wanted everyone to have free access to the contributions of this individual. The place you donate to will offer you a statement for tax purposes. However, it's up to you or your accountant to give it a dollar value.

Funeral Program and Obituary

The funeral program is a very important document as is the obituary. Be sure the facts and spellings are correct. The information they contain is a history for that loved one's personal, professional, and genealogical data for present and future generations.

Take the time with your loved one to write both if at all possible. It will be the most fitting final honor for your loved one.

Funeral Planning

THE REALITY OF LIFE is that, once we are born, we will die. This sounds harsh, and most of us would much rather not talk about it. But eventually it becomes necessary. Thinking about your own funeral plans so that loved ones know your wishes is a wonderful gift to your family. And you should definitely discuss this with other family members, old and young. While they probably haven't given it any thought, this could start them to focus on an inevitable situation for someone to implement. At the time of their death, plans have to be made. It is helpful if those plans have been expressed to someone in the family or plans are stated in a Will. If a person has a Will, inquire with the lawyer whether there are any special instructions for burial.

> *Personal Experience: On many occasions, Mother discussed who she wanted on her funeral program but never talked about or prearranged her funeral necessities. Things changed when she finally agreed to attend my younger aunt's funeral. The decision was difficult for her because she didn't want to be sad or cause her daughters an inconvenience with her wheelchair. She was assured the funeral wouldn't be sad and the funeral director had resolved her concerns regarding the wheelchair. In addition, her caregiver would be by her side.*
>
> *After this service she pulled me aside and asked me to plan her funeral with the same service as my aunt had. She was pleased and happy she went. Now, she was ready to make plans for her own funeral details.*

ANSWER FOR YOURSELF the following questions, and then discuss your desires with loved ones. Ask them whether they have determined what they would desire for themselves. The recommended time to discuss this is before your loved one or you have a life-changing situation.

- Do you want to be buried or cremated?
- Where do you want to be buried, or what is to be done with your ashes?

- Do you want a funeral in a church, services at a chapel, by the gravesite, no service, or memorial service?
- What type of service do you want?
- What funeral establishment do you wish to use?

The key to answering these questions will be determined by one's finances. One should research for viable area funeral homes to determine your options. In addition, asking close friends about their funeral home experiences can help you to create a list of places to visit—and not visit—for meetings with funeral directors. Do check with the Better Business Bureau to see whether and what complaints may have been filed against the funeral establishment.

When exploring options, you should get to know these businesses and the cost of services they offer. Be prepared during your appointment to hear things you never thought of being discussed. The information you are being given is best discussed sooner rather than later when emotions are fragile.

The Funeral or Memorial Service

IDEALLY, YOU WERE ABLE to discuss whom your loved one wanted on the program for his or her funeral or memorial service. If you had this discussion, do your best to abide by your relative's wishes. Many people, however, don't want to talk about their deaths. If you didn't discuss the matter with your loved one before he or she died, you are at liberty to create the program yourself.

After you've established a date for the service, call the desired people, and ask them if they can be a part of the program. If they decline or are unavailable select another person whom you think knew your loved one. The religious leader may also be able to suggest participants.

If you are not familiar with the program order for a service at your loved one's place of worship, the religious leader can help you. Most religious leaders—as well as funeral directors—will be eager to accommodate your wishes. If you decide to hold the service at a nonreligious venue, there are books that can help you with planning. *(See page 193: Memorial Service Planning Resources.)*

Select and safely store family photographs you wish to include on the printed program. Remembering where they are may be a challenge. When death comes, your brain may shut down, and your fragile emotional state may make it hard to get things done, so please plan ahead.

Journal

Approaching Death Tasks

- **How much biographical information do I have on the family member?**

_____

_____

_____

- **Where can I get a photograph of the family member?**

_____

_____

- **Where were they born?**

_____

- **When were they born?**

Month	Day	Year

- **Where did they work?**

- **Worship?**

- **Volunteer?**

• *What are some memorable moments in the family member's life?*

_____

_____

_____

_____

_____

_____

_____

• *List the full name of immediate family members and spouses.*

_____

_____

_____

_____

_____

_____

_____

• *When will the services be held?*

Date   Time
_____   _____

Place
_____

What is the family's desire regarding flowers and donations?
_____

Flowers: ☐ Yes   ☐ No
_____

If no, where should donations be sent in lieu of flowers?
_____

_____

_____

• *Additional notes:*

_____

_____

_____

_____

_____

_____

_____

Chapter Twenty

Death and Dying

The troubles of my heart have multiplied; free me from my anguish.
— Psalm 25:17

Dealing with Grief

GRIEVING AFTER YOUR LOVED ONE DIES is as natural as feeling joy when something wonderful happens. In fact, the joy and love that you can no longer share with your loved one is part of why you're grieving. Joy and love are a gift, and in a sense, so is grief. It is important, therefore, to honor each emotion you experience.

People are different and so are the ways in which they grieve. You may experience many emotions and behaviors. In fact, you may experience varying emotions simultaneously, and they can arise at anytime, anywhere. Regrettably, you may not be able to control your emotions, so embrace them. Eventually, they will subside.

The family should be aware of the different mental stages of death and dying, so you will know what to expect. These mental stages begin when doctors have done all they can to cure a loved one medically.

The description of three models for stages of dying and stages of grief are listed below.

Dr. Elisabeth Kübler-Ross, a psychiatrist who led the way to developing descriptions for these emotions, identified the following five psychological stages in loss experiences.

- Denial (shock and numbness)
- Anger
- Bargaining
- Depression
- Acceptance[1]

Dr. J. William Worden, professor of psychology, is considered the father of parish nursing and the founder of The International Parish Nurse Resource Center in St. Louis, Missouri. Dr. Worden created a list of descriptions of the stages in the dying and grief process called the *Four Tasks of Mourning.* These are the primary source for the hospice services as they help people through the stages of their grief.

His list includes these four steps:

- The survivor is to accept the reality of the loss.
- The survivor is to work through the pain of the loss.
- The survivor is to adjust to the environment in which the person is missing.
- The survivor is to relocate and memorialize the life.[2]

Rev. Granger Westberg, a Lutheran minister, developed ten steps in the dying and grieving process. Westberg believes people repeat the first eight steps over and over before they reach the last two steps.

His steps include:

- Shock and denial
- Anger/resentment
- Panic
- Depression and loneliness
- Hope
- Emotional eruption
- Illness/physical symptoms
- Guilt
- Reentry difficulties
- Affirming reality[3]

---

1 Kübler-Ross, Elisabeth. *On Death and Dying,* NY: Simon & Schuster, 1997.
2 Bowen, Debra and Strickler, Susan. *A Good Friend for Bad Times: Helping Others Through Grief,* Augsburg Fortress Publishers: Minneapolis, MN, 2004.
3 Retired Pastor of the Evangelical Lutheran Church in America (ELCA).

Strategies for dealing with grief:

- Give yourself permission to cry.
- Cry when you feel like crying.
- Offer others your shoulders to cry on.
- Talk about your loved one, and what they meant to you.
- Listen to others talk to you about the loved one.
- Share funny stories of experiences with loved one. These can brighten the bereavement experience.
- Saying a soft "I love you" to another family member could cheer them up. Many times this is all that's needed.

What to Do When Death Occurs

WHAT YOU DO depends on the situation of the death. Different situations warrant different actions. The more informed you are as to these procedures, the less chaotic this emotional time will be.

- **When your loved one passes away at home,** you should call the doctor, or 911, or the coroner's office and you may expect that they will call the police. Once the person is pronounced dead by a professional, call the funeral home of your choice to pick up the body. The funeral director will make arrangements to register the death and will talk with you soon after to make an appointment to discuss funeral arrangements.

- **When a person dies in a hospital,** the doctor or head nurse on duty will call you to come to the hospital. The on-duty doctor should sign the death certificate.

- When a person expires in a health facility, the head nurse or doctor on duty will notify you. They or you can call the funeral home designated in the deceased's file that was submitted upon admittance to that facility.

- **When the death occurs out of state,** you will need to call your funeral director immediately. They should be able to make transportation arrangements for the deceased. It is important to remember this because they have a contact for out-of-state pickups that is less costly than a funeral home in that location picking up the body. You will be charged twice—once for the original pickup, and once for transportation to the funeral home you have chosen.

Once the body has been retrieved, there are tasks to be done immediately. First, make calls to essential family members. Usually family members will share in calling other family members at the appropriate time. And they will volunteer to call friends of the deceased if you provide contact information.

However, you should call at least these people:

- Close relatives of the deceased
- Employer and fellow employees
- The deceased's insurance company or insurance agent
- Family doctor
- Cemetery or other burial site—this call could be made by the funeral director once you meet to make funeral arrangements
- Organizations the deceased belonged to—for example, a church, fraternal group, social club such as Elks, Lion's Club, Toastmasters

If your loved one dies at a hospital, nursing home, or hospice center, the facility will allow the body to remain in place so that close relatives—usually immediate family members—can view the body before it is taken to a funeral home. Sometimes, however, viewing the body is not advised. If this is the case, the medical personnel will tell you.

After you have notified close relatives and your loved one's religious leader, these additional details should be addressed:

- Collect personal valuables and belongings right away, if the death occurred at a health facility.
- Look for prearranged funeral plans and contracts.
- Secure life insurance policy—it may cover funeral costs.
- Make an appointment with the funeral director to discuss your service needs.
- Inform the Social Security Administration of your loved one's death (if he or she collected Social Security payments). Having payments stopped immediately will prevent you from having to return money.

> **Note:** If your loved one was the victim of a crime, the coroner's office will pick up the body for an autopsy. Once the autopsy is completed, the body will be delivered to a funeral home.

Making Final Arrangements

WHEN MAKING THE final arrangements for your loved one, only the most necessary people should be involved in this process. Emotions are fragile during this time. Decision-making will be easier if you involve as few people as possible.

As part of the meeting, discuss the following:
- Date and place for the funeral or memorial service
- Details for the wake/viewing and the funeral
- Clothing for the deceased and other items needed to prepare the body for the funeral
- Death certificates (order multiple copies to resolve business issues—e.g., filing insurance claims and closing bank accounts)

Tip: Tell the funeral director what your budget is and stay within it. The funeral director can offer suggestions but you must manage the finances.

Post-Service Details

AFTER THE FUNERAL or memorial service, you will need to perform other tasks before and after family members return home. After-service tasks may include:
- Giving an honorarium to the religious leader, special musicians, and technical staff who performed at the service.
- Sending thank-you cards to people who sent flowers, provided food for the family, rendered personal services, and attended the viewing. Remember to include out-of-towners who attended the funeral service.
- Sending thank-you letters or cards to participants in the service who were not acknowledged with an honorarium.
- Removing the loved one's personal items from their home or place of residence, especially if no Will was drawn.

Legal Matters—After Death

AFTER YOUR LOVED one has died, his or her Last Will and Testament *(See Appendix C: Sample Legal Documents)* will need to be settled. As Power of Attorney holder, your responsibilities end when your loved one passes away, the POA is no longer legally valid. You will need to:
- Locate and read the Will to find out who's been named the Executor or Executrix if you don't already know.
- Give the original notarized Will to the Executor or Executrix.
- Keep your loved one's tangible belongings—this is not the time to give them away.
- Be patient. The waiting period before a loved one's Will can be probated varies. It takes 45 days in some states.

Things you should know about the probate process:

- What are the specifics of the Will?
- What is the value of the estate? In some states, only estates greater than $25,000 are probated. In that instance a lawyer is required.
- If you do not have the original notarized Will, a lawyer will be required to verify with the heirs the authenticity of the document.
- The Will has to be dealt with through probate court in the state where the deceased was domiciled.
- Call the local probate court clerk to determine what is required for your loved one's jurisdiction.
- Usually, the Executor or Executrix must appear in court to be questioned by the probate judge and sworn in.

Tip: Only discuss "the facts" about the process of probating the Will with family members because emotions may still be soaring.

Journal
Death and Dying

- **What comforts me most when I feel sad?**

_____

_____

_____

_____

- **These are the names and contact information of people I should call when my loved one passes.**

_____

_____

_____

_____

_____

_____

- *If discussed with loved one, what service desires did they prefer?*

_____

_____

_____

_____

- *If not discussed, what do I think they would have wanted at their service?*

_____

_____

_____

_____

- *Do I have all the facts of my loved one's life such as exact dates of birth, employment, spouse, children, etc.?*

_____

_____

_____

• *What family member do I want to help me plan the service?*

_____

_____

• *What is the budget and source for financing the service or memorial?*

_____

_____

• *Who is on the program and what honorarium do I give them?*

_____

_____

• *Where is the file for death-related policies, and Last Will and Testament?*

_____

_____

• *What needs to be done right away?*

_____

_____

- *Additional notes:*

Afterword

THE KNOWLEDGE AND NURSING EXPERIENCE of Dr. Carr, along with my care-giving experiences and those of family and my friends are shared throughout *Stepping Up*. Our journeys through these experiences, coupled with the knowledge we acquired, made us more grateful for life and all of its complexities. Your journey could be similar, or it may be totally different, but the information in this book should help you as to meet the challenges of being a family caregiver.

Whether you are a 'Boomer', 'Generation X', or 'Generation Y', your journey caring for loved ones will be less challenging and less painful by talking to your family and friends NOW about their wishes should they encounter a life-changing experience. These experiences happen without warning and you as family caregiver must ensure that you are *Stepping Up*.

Again, we wish you patience, perseverance, and love for you and your loved one. Remember to be thankful that you are alive and able to care for someone, as opposed to them taking care of you.

—Cenetta J. Lee
Southport, North Carolina
January 2012

Appendix A:
Resources for Information

Books

Cancer Resources

American Cancer Society. *Cancer Caregiving A- Z. An At-Home Guide for Patients and Families.* 2008.

Caregiving Resources

Abramson, Alexis. *The Caregiver's Survival Handbook: How to Care for Your Aging Parent Without Losing Yourself.* 2004.

American Medical Association. *American Medical Association Guide to Home Caregiving.* 2001.

Berman, Claire. *Caring for Yourself While Caring for Your Aging Parents.* 2005.

Delehanty, Hugh and Ginzler, Elinor. *Caring for Your Parents.* 2005.

Delehanty, Hugh, Elinor Ginzler, and Mary Pipher. *Caring for Your Parents: The Complete Family Guide (AARP).* 2008.

Hennessey, Maya. *If Only I'd Had This Caregiving Book.* 2006.

Houts, Peter. *Caregiving (2nd ed.).* 2003.

Knutson, Lois. *Compassionate Caregiving: Practical Help and Spiritual Encouragement for Caregivers.* 2007.

Loverde, Joy. *The Complete Eldercare Planner: Where to Start, Which Questions to Ask, and How to Find Help.* 2009.

Loverde, Joy. *The Complete Eldercare Planner, Revised and Updated Edition: Where to Start, Which Questions to Ask, and How to Find Help.* 2009.

Morris, Virginia. *How to Care for Aging Parents (2nd ed.).* 2004.

Quan, Kathy. *Everything Guide to Caring for Aging Parents.* 2009.

Spring, Janis Abrahms. *Life with Pop: Lessons on Caring for An Aging Parent.* 2009.

Decluttering Resources

Coggins, Beverly. *1-2-3… Get Organized Series: Three Steps to Decluttering.* 2007.

Good Housekeeping Clutter Rescue: Just Minutes a Day to Get Organized Forever. *2008.*

Leeds, Regina. *The Complete Idiot's Guide to Decluttering.* 2007.

Dementia Resources

Brooker, Dawn. *Person-Centered Dementia Care: Making Services Better.* 2007.

Mace, Nancy and Peter V. *Rabins.* The 36-Hour Day: Guide for People with Alzheimer Disease, Other Dementias, and Memory Loss in Late Life. 2006.

Radin, Lisa. *What If It's Not Alzheimer's: A Caregiver's Guide to Dementia.* 2008.

McCurry, M. *Susan.* When a Family Member Has Dementia: Steps to Becoming a Resilient Caregiver. 2006.

Fell, Naomi. *The Validation Breakthrough: Simple Techniques for Communicating with People with Alzheimer's Type Dementia.* 2002.

Gibbons, Leeza, James Huysman and Rosemary DeAngelis Laird. *One with Memory Loss.* (2009).

Bazan-Salazar, Emilia. *Alzheimer's Activities that Stimulate the Mind.* 2005.

Glenner, Joy A., *Jean M.* Stehman, Margaret J. Galante, Martha L. Green, and Judith Davagnino. When Your Loved One has Dementia: A Simple Guide for Caregivers. 2005.

Callone, Patricia, Janaan Manternach, Roger Brumback, Roger Brumbeck and Connie Kudlacek. *A Caregiver's Guide to Alzheimer's: 300 Tips for Making Life Easier.* 2006.

Brackey, Jolene. *Creating Moments of Joy for the Person with Alzheimer's or Dementia.* 2008.

Eldercare Resources

Epstein, Lita. *The 250 Eldercare Questions Everyone Should Ask.* 2009.

Hall, Julie. *The Boomer Burden: Dealing with Your Parents' Lifetime Accumulation of Stuff.* 2008.

Beerman, Susan and Judith Rappaport-Musson. *Eldercare 911 Question and Answer Book.* 2005.

Rantz, Marilyn. *How to Find the Best Eldercare.* 2009.

Zukerman, Rachelle. *Eldercare for Dummies.* 2003.

Family Relations Resources

Brinkman, Rick and Rick Kirschner. *Dealing With Relatives (…even if you can't stand them): Bringing Out the Best in Families at Their Worst (Paperback).* 2002.

Fleder, Leonard, Ph.D. *When Difficult Relatives Happen to Good People: Surviving Your Family and Keeping Your Sanity (Paperback).* 2005.

Funeral Planning Resources

Abraham, Melissa. *When We Remember: Inspiration and Integrity for a Meaningful Funeral.* 2007.

Bailey, Susan and Carmen Flowers. *Grave Expectations: Planning the End Like There's No Tomorrow.* 2009.

Breuhaus, Betty. *When the Sun Goes Down: Serendipitous Guide to Planning Your Own Funeral.* 2007.

Carnell, Geoffrey. *Complete Guide to Funeral Planning: How to Arrange the Appropriate Service.* 2004.

Cochrane, Don S., *Simply Essential Funeral Planning Kit.* 2002.

Llewellyn, John F., *Saying Goodbye Your Way: Planning or Buying a Funeral or Cremation for Yourself or Someone You Love.* 2004.

Grief Resources

- ### *Adults*

Albom, Mitch. *Tuesday with Morrie: An Old Man, a Young Man, and Life's Greatest Lesson.* 2002.

Heegaard, Marge Eaton. *When Someone Very Special Dies: Children Can Learn to Cope with Grief.* 1988.

Hickman, Martha. *Healing After Loss: Daily Meditations for Working Through Grief.* 1999.

James, John W., Russell Friedman. *The Grief Recovery Handbook, 20th Anniversary Expanded Edition: The Action Program for Moving Beyond Death, Divorce, and Other Losses including Health, Career, and Faith. 2003.*

Katafiasz, Karen. *Grief Therapy.* 1993.

Kübler-Ross, Elisabeth. *Questions and Answers on Death and Dying.* 1999.

Kübler-Ross, Elisabeth and David Kussler. *On Grief and Grieving: Finding Meaning of Grief Through the Five Stages of Loss.* 2007.

Leming, Michael R. and George E. Dickinson. *Understanding Dying, Death, and Bereavement.* 2006.

O'Malley, William. *Yielding Prayers for Those in Need of Hope.* 1992.

Walton, Charlie. *When There Are No Words: Finding Your Way to Cope with Loss and Grief.* 1996.

Westburg, Granger. *Good Grief.* 2004.

Wolfeit, Alan D. *Understanding Your Grief: Ten Essential Touchstones for Finding Hope and Healing Your Heart.* 2004.

• *Children*—Ages 4-8

Mellonie, Bryan, and Ingpen, Robert. *Lifetimes.* 1983.

Ryan, Victoria. *When Your Grandparent Dies: A Child's Guide to Good Grief.* 2002.

Schweibert, Pat. *Tear Soup: A Recipe for Healing After Loss.* 2005.

Shriver, Maria. *What's Heaven? 1999.*

Silverman, Janis. *Help Me Say Goodbye: Activities for Helping Kids Cope When a Special Person Dies.* 1999.

Simon, Norma. *The Saddest Time.* 1992.

Thomas, Pat. *I Miss You: A First Look at Death.* 2001.

• *Children*—Ages 9-12

Heegard, Marge. *When Someone Very Special Dies.* 1988.

Legal Resources

Alexander, George J., *Writing a Living Will: Using a Durable Power-of-Attorney.* 1987.

Bove, Alexander A., *The Complete Book of Wills, Estates and Trusts.* 2005.

Larson, Aaron. *Will and Trusts Kits for Dummies.* 2005.

Orman, Suze. *Suze Orman's Will and Trust Kit: The Ultimate Protection Portfolio.* 2007.

Palermo, Michael. *AARP Crash Course in Estate Planning.* 2004.

Ventura, John. *Kiplinger's Estate planning: The Complete Guide to Wills, Trusts, and Maximizing Your Legacy.* 2008.

Sitarz, Daniel. *Advanced Health Care Directives Simplified.* 2007.

Sitarz, Daniel. *Powers-of-Attorney Simplified.* 2007.

Memorial Service Planning Resources

Bennett, Amanda & Foley, Terrence. *In Memoriam: A Practical Guide to Planning a Memorial Service.* 1997.

Moore, Faith & Baldridge, Letitia. *Celebrating a Life: Planning Memorial Services & Other Creative Remembrances.* 2009.

Searl, Edward. *In Memoriam: A Guide to Modern Funeral and Memorial Services.* 2000.

Nursing Home Resources

Heiser, K. Gabriel. *How To Protect Your Family's Assets from Devastating Nursing Home Costs: Medicaid Secrets.* 2008.

Mills, S. *Your Guide to Choosing A Nursing Home.* (Kindle Edition). 2009.

Webb, Mary. *Choosing a Nursing Home to Arrange the Right Long-term Care for the Elderly.* 1996.

Physician Relationship Resources

American Medical Association. *American Medical Association Guide to Talking to Your Doctor.* 2001.

Stress Management Resources

Davis, Martha, Elizabeth Robbins Eshelman, Matthew McKay, and Patrick Fanning. *The Relaxation & Stress Reduction Workbook.* 2008.

Epstein, Robert. *The Big Book of Stress Relief Games: Quick, Fun Activities for Feeling Better.* 2000.

Hoffmann, David. *An Herbal Guide to Stress Relief: Gentle Remedies and Techniques for Healing and Calming the Nervous System.* 1991.

Lazarus, Judith. *Stress Relief & Relaxation Techniques.* 2000.

Stebnicki, Mark A., *Empathy Fatigue: Healing the Mind,Body, and Spirit of Professional Counselors.* 2008.

Internet Resources

- ## *Websites*

www.aarp.org (American Association of Retired Persons)

www.adt.com (ADT Home Security)

www.aoa.gov (Administration on Aging)

www.cancer.com (Cancer.*Com*)

www.cancer.gov (National Cancer Institute)

www.caregiving.org (Family Caregiver Alliance – National Center on Caregiving)

www.caremanager.org (National Professional Association of Geriatric Care Managers)

www.caregiverslibrary.org (National Caregivers Library)

www.elderlawanswers.com (Elderlawnet, Inc.)

www.familydoctor.org (Family Doctor)

www.harthosp.org (Hartford Hospital Stroke Center)

www.medicalert.org (MedicAlert Foundation)

www.medicare.org (Medicare Information Source)

www.medlineplus.gov (U.S. National Library of Medicine and National Institutes of Health

www.nhpco.org (National Hospice and Palliative Care Organization)

www.nih.gov (National Institutes of Health)

www.nfcacares.org.com (National Family Caregivers Association)

www.usa.gov (United States of America Government)

www.webmd.com (WebMD)

www.americanheart.org (American Heart Association)

www.stroke.org (National Stroke Association)

www.strokeassociation.org (American Stroke Association)

www.fte.gov (Federal Trade Commission)

www.va.gov (United States Department of Veteran Affairs)

Appendix B:
Tips for Searching the Internet

Tips for Searching the Internet

FINDING INFORMATION on the Internet is involved and challenging for all of us. *As a librarian, I acknowledge the importance of researching a topic using a vast database such as the Internet.* To make your search for information easier, faster, and more productive, I have included the following tips on searching the Internet. Also, I have included helpful books, websites and other caregiver resources on my website at *www.eclecticcaring.com.*

The Internet offers information at your fingertips immediately. The key to using the Internet is the search. Databases are available on your computer to do the searches for you. However, for optimal searches use Google, Yahoo and Bing.

- Think of as many words that express what you are looking for and type these in the Google search box, example—caregivers, caretakers, etc.
- To search for closely related terms, you may employ "wildcards." For example, suppose you wanted to search for websites containing either the term *neurosurgery* or the term *neurosurgical.* Simply type into your Google search box: *neurosurg*.* The asterisk tells your search engine to look for any word beginning with *neurosurg-,* including both *neurosurgery and neurosurgical.*

You may type the question you want to have answered in the Google search box. For example, *"How do I care for an ill person?"* Describe what you want with as few words as possible because each word you use will be searched on the Web.

Narrow your search by adding words. Just type in whatever comes to your mind, for example—*personal care, home care, home nursing, nursing care, nursing home, medical care at home,* etc.

Narrow it down to only the pages with the exact phrase. For example, "caregiving at home." *Be ready to try close alternatives.* If you don't get what you want by searching "caregiving," for example, use the search term *care giving* or (with quotes) *"care giving".*

Search for these terms at the same time—for example—*"caregiving"* or *"home care".*

You can search for a service or topic linked with a particular city or state— for example, by typing in as a pair of Google search terms *"nursing homes"* and *"Minneapolis".*

A few keys for reading the results that may come up in your search...

WHEN YOU FIND one entry on your screen's left margin and another indented just beneath it, the indented version is an alternate address for the very same website.

In each entry, you'll find that the webpage title is on the first line. *An excerpt from the webpage often referred to as a snippet.* The webpage address is also known as the Uniform Resource Locator (URL). Next is a link to the webpage with more information also known as *cached links*. The top row of the web page offers specific searches, such as maps, images, news, etc.

Beyond topical searches, do consult directly the websites of community health agencies and state and federal government agencies you may know that provide special services to the elderly and others.

Appendix C:
Sample Legal Documents

In this section, you will find samples of the legal documents that will help you as you assume caregiver responsibilities. It is important that you verify that you have the most current version of the legal document before you take any action. You can check with a lawyer, legal aid or the appropriate government agency.

THIS IS AN EXAMPLE ONLY.
Durable Power of Attorney for may vary from case to case and state to state.
GRANTOR'S NAME
DURABLE POWER OF ATTORNEY

KNOW all men by these presents that I, _____, the undersigned, of _____, do hereby make, constitute and appoint _____, _____, my true and lawful attorney-in-fact, to do and perform all things that I could do myself in the transaction of any business of mine, on such terms and in such manner as said attorney-in-fact may deem appropriate, including without limitation, power and authority:

1. TO EXERCISE or perform any act, power, duty, right or obligation whatsoever that I now have, or may hereafter acquire the legal right, power or capacity to exercise or perform, in connection with, arising from, or relating to any person, item, transaction, thing, business property, real or personal, tangible or intangible, or matter whatsoever;

2. TO OPEN, maintain and close checking and savings accounts in my name in any banks, savings and loan associations, building and loan associations, credit unions, or similar institutions; to receive, endorse and deposit negotiable instruments made or drawn to my order; to issue, receive or endorse with my name checks, drafts, and orders for the payment of money from, or to any account of mine in any such institution, including those payable to said attorney-in-fact; to agree to and sign in my name any authority, signature cards or other documents that my attorney-in-fact or any institution may deem appropriate; to lease, maintain and close out safe deposit boxes in any banking or other institution, and to enter any safe deposit box or place of safekeeping of property now or hereafter maintained in my name or on my behalf without anyone else being present, and

to agree to and sign in my name any authority, signature cards or other documents for such purposes;

3. TO REQUEST, claim, demand, sue for, recover, collect, receive, and hold and possess all such sums of money, debts, dues, commercial paper, checks, drafts, accounts, deposits, legacies, bequests, devises, notes, interests, stock certificates, bonds, dividends, certificates of deposit, annuities, demands, pension and retirement benefits, insurance benefits and proceeds, any and all documents of title, choses in action, personal and real property, intangible and tangible property and property rights and demands whatsoever, liquidated or unliquidated, as now are, or shall hereafter become, owned by, or due, owing, payable, or belonging to, me or in which I have or may hereafter acquire interest, to have, use, and take all lawful ways and means and equitable and legal remedies, procedures, and writs in my name for the collection and recovery thereof, and to adjust, sell, compromise, forgive and agree for the same, and to make, execute and deliver for me, on my behalf, and in my name, all endorsements, acquittances, releases, receipts or other sufficient discharges for the same;

4. TO LEASE, purchase, sell, exchange and acquire, and to agree, bargain, and contract for the lease, purchase, sale, exchange and acquisition of, and to accept, take, receive and possess any real or personal property whatsoever, tangible or intangible, or interest thereon, and including but not limited to all types of stocks and bonds and other similar kinds of securities;

5. TO MAINTAIN, repair, improve, manage, insure, rent, lease, sell, convey, subject to liens, mortgage, subject to deeds of trust, and hypothecate, and in any way or manner deal with all or any part of any real or personal property whatsoever, tangible or intangible, or any interest therein, that I now own or may hereafter acquire, for me, in my behalf, and in my name and under such terms and conditions, and under such covenants, as said attorney-in-fact shall deem proper;

6. TO MAKE, receive, sign, endorse, execute, acknowledge, deliver and possess such applications, contracts, agreements, options, covenants, conveyances, deeds, trust deeds, security agreements, bills of sale, leases, mortgages, assignments, insurance policies, bills of lading, warehouse receipts, documents of title, bills, bonds, debentures, checks, drafts, bills of exchange, letters of credit, notes, stock certificates, proxies, warrants, commercial paper, receipts, withdrawal receipts and deposit instruments relating to accounts or deposits in, or certificates of deposit of, bans, savings and loan or other institutions or associations, proofs of loss, evidences of debts, releases, and satisfaction of mortgages,

liens, judgments, security agreements and other debts and obligations and such other instruments in writing of whatever kind and nature as may be necessary or proper in the exercise of the rights and powers herein granted. This shall include the powers to deal with retirement plans, including IRA rollovers and voluntary contributions; to borrow funds in order to avoid forced liquidation of assets; power to deal with life insurance; to enter buy-sell agreements, and to pay salaries of employees;

7. TO MAKE and sign in my name any and all tax or other returns to the State or Federal Government or other taxing authority; to request extensions in connection with such taxes, to protest in my name any such taxes or the proposed assessment of any such taxes; to file claims for refunds of taxes; to sign IRS powers of attorney; to settle tax disputes; and to make statutory elections and disclaimers;

8. TO ENTER any personal appearance for me as a plaintiff or as a defendant in any legal action, suit, court, or hearing or to accept, waive or acknowledge any process or service of process from any court, board or agency whatsoever directed to me personally; and to compromise, refer to arbitration, or submit to judgment in any such action or proceeding;

9. TO MAKE gifts or fund inter vivos trusts with any of my assets to any individuals, and/or to any charities, provided that I have previously made gifts to such donee, or such donee is a beneficiary under my most recently executed Will, as determined by my attorney-in-fact, or such donee is otherwise a natural object of my bounty; and to complete any charitable pledges which I may make;

10. TO TRANSFER any or all of my assets to a trustee to hold same in trust upon such terms and conditions as my attorney-in-fact may deem appropriate, provided such trust (a) is solely for my benefit; (b) may be amended or revoked by me or my attorney-in-fact; and (c) provides that at my death all assets then held in such trust shall be delivered to the personal representative of my estate;

11. TO EMPLOY and compensate attorneys-at-law, accountants, real estate agents, and other such agents and advisors with relation to any matters mentioned herein;

12. TO CONTRACT with or employ any person or institution for the purpose of caring for me, as my said attorney-in-fact may deem necessary or desirable, and to pay any expenses in connection therewith out of my funds;

13. TO CONDUCT, engage in, and transact any and all lawful business of whatever nature or kind for me, on my behalf, and in my name.

I GRANT TO said attorney-in-fact full power and authority to do, take, and perform all and every act and thing whatsoever requisite, proper or necessary to be done, in the exercise of any of the rights and powers herein granted, as fully to all intents and purposes as I might or could do if personally present, with full power of substitution or revocation, hereby ratifying and confirming all that said attorney-in-fact, or his substitute or substitutes, shall lawfully do or cause to be done by virtue of this power of attorney and the rights and powers herein granted.

THIS INSTRUMENT IS to be construed and interpreted as a general power of attorney. The enumeration of specific items, rights, acts, or powers herein is not intended to, nor does it, limit or restrict, and is not to be construed or interpreted as limiting or restricting, the general powers herein granted to said attorney-in-fact.

THE RIGHTS, POWERS and authority of said attorney-in-fact herein granted shall commence and be in full force and effect on the date of execution until terminated by me on written notice.

   THIS POWER IS TO BE CONSTRUED AS A DURABLE POWER OF ATTORNEY UNDER SECTION _____. *THIS POWER OF ATTORNEY SHALL NOT BE AFFECTED OR TERMINATED BY MY SUBSEQUENT DISABILITY OR INCAPACITY OR INCOMPETENCY.*

   Dated this _____ day of _____, 20xx.

   _____

   Grantor's Signature

   STATE OF _____

   COUNTY OF _____

I HEREBY CERTIFY that on this day before me, an officer duly authorized in the state aforesaid and in the county aforesaid to take acknowledgments, personally appeared _____, known to me to be the person described in and who executed the foregoing instrument and acknowledged before me that (s)he executed the same.

WITNESS MY HAND and official seal in the county and state last aforesaid this_____ day of _____, 20xx.

_____

Notary Public

My Commission Expires: _____

This IS AN EXAMPLE ONLY. Durable Power of Attorney for Healthcare may vary from case to case and state to state.

DURABLE POWER OF ATTORNEY FOR HEALTH CARE

I.

DESIGNATION OF HEALTH CARE AGENT

KNOW all men by these presents that I, _____, the undersigned, this document, (as evidenced by the warning statement read by me and attached hereto) do hereby make, constitute and appoint _____, of _____, my Agent to act for me and in my name, place and stead, and on my behalf, and for my use and benefit, in all situations involving health care decisions concerning me, hereby revoking any prior durable power of attorney for health care previously signed by me. *If I no longer have the capacity to make health care decisions for myself, I hereby grant to my Agent full power and authority to make health care decisions for me to the same extent that I could make such decisions for myself if I had the capacity to do so.* My incapacity to make health care decisions for myself shall be certified in of _____, with full knowledge of the effect of writing by my treating physician and confirmed by a second physician who has personally examined me. In exercising this authority, I request my Agent to make health care decisions that are consistent with my desires as stated in this document or which I have otherwise made known to him/her.

II.

POWERS AND AUTHORITY OF HEALTH CARE AGENTS

The authorization granted herein shall include, but not be limited to the power and/or right to:

A. *Determine visitation privileges within a hospital or other medical facility and be notified in case of any emergency or change in medical condition;*

B. *Employ and discharge medical personnel, including physicians, psychologists, dentists, nurses, therapists and other health care providers as my Agent shall deem necessary for my physical, mental and emotional well-being and to pay them or cause them to be paid reasonable compensation;*

C. *Take whatever steps are necessary or advisable, including employment of round-the-clock nursing care, to allow me to remain in my personal residence as long as is determined by my Agent to be reasonable in the circumstances;*

D. Give or withhold consent to any medical procedure, test or treatment including surgical procedures; to arrange for my hospitalization, convalescent care, hospice or home care; to summon paramedics or other emergency medical personnel and seek emergency treatment for me, as my Agent deems appropriate; and under circumstances in which my Agent determines that certain medical procedures, tests or treatments are no longer of any benefit to me, or where the benefits are outweighed by the burdens imposed, to revoke, withdraw, modify or change consent to such procedures, tests and treatments, as well as hospitalization, convalescent care, hospice or home care, which I or my Agent may have previously allowed or consented to or which may have been implied due to emergency conditions; to make decisions regarding use of such drugs or procedures that may lead to permanent physical damage, or addiction, or may hasten the moment of my death, or be against conventional medical advice.

My Agent's decision shall be guided by:

(1) The provisions of this document;

(2) Any reliable evidence or preferences that I may have expressed on the subject, whether before or after the execution of this document;

(3) What my Agent believes I would want done in the circumstances if I were able to express myself;

(4) Any information given to my Agent by the treating physician as to my medical diagnosis and prognosis and the intrusiveness, pain, risks and side effects associated with the treatment, and any treatment or course of action recommended to my Agent by such treating physicians;

I have this date executed an AUTHORIZATION FOR USE AND DISCLOSURE OF PROTECTED HEALTH INFORMATION authorizing my Agent to obtain medical information that may be protected under the privacy rules of 45 CFR § 164.

E. *Make all decisions concerning donation of any organs where my death might become imminent or having already come about, and to direct or consent that an autopsy be undertaken.* I hereby direct the Executor of my estate and my family to respect my Agent's decision in this regard.

F. *(1) Obtain medical and health care records and any other information regarding my physical or mental health; (2) execute on my behalf any releases or other documents that may be required in order to obtain such information; (3) consent to the disclosure of such information to others; (4) execute any document necessary to implement health care decisions made by my Agent; and (5) execute any waiver or release from liability that my Agent determines to be appropriate.*

G. *Make all decisions involving burial and funeral arrangements.* The rights, powers and authority of said Agent herein granted shall commence and be in full force and effect on the date of execution until terminated by me.

III.

THIRD PARTY RELIANCE

For the purpose of inducing individuals, organizations, and entities (including, but not limited to, any physician, hospital, nursing home, health care provider, insurer, or other person, all of whom will be referred to in this Article as a "person") to act in accordance with the instructions of my Agent as authorized in this document, I hereby represent, warrant and agree that:

A. *Reliance on Agent's Authority and Representations.* No person who relies in good faith upon the authority of my Agent under this document shall incur any liability to me, my estate, my heirs, successors or assigns. In addition, no person who relies in good faith upon any representation my Agent may make as to: (1) the fact that my Agent's powers are then in effect, (2) the scope of my Agent's authority granted under this document, (3) my competency at the time this document is executed, (4) the fact that this document has not been revoked, or (5) the fact that my Agent continues to serve as my Agent shall not incur any liability to me, my estate, my heirs, successors or assigns for permitting my Agent to exercise any such authority.

B. *No Liability for Unknown Revocation or Amendment.* If this document is revoked or amended for any reason, I, my estate, my heirs, successors and assigns will hold any person harmless from any loss suffered or liability incurred as a result of such person acting in good faith upon the instructions of my Agent prior to the receipt by such person of actual notice of such revocation or amendment.

C. *Agent May Act Alone.* The powers conferred on my Agent by this document may be exercised by my Agent alone, and my Agent's signature or act under the authority granted in this document may be accepted by persons as fully authorized by me and with the same force and effect as if I were personally present, competent and acting on my own behalf. Consequently, all acts lawfully done by my Agent hereunder are done with my consent and shall have the same validity and effect as if I were personally present and personally exercised the powers myself, and shall inure to the benefit of and bind me, my estate, my heirs, successors, assigns, and personal representatives.

D. Release of Information. I hereby authorize all physicians who have treated health care, including psychologists and hospitals, to release to my me, and all other providers of Agent all information or photocopies of any records that my Agent may request. If I am incompetent at the time my Agent requests such information, all persons are authorized to treat any such request for information by my Agent as the request of my legal representative and to honor such request on that basis. I hereby waive all privileges that may be applicable to such information and records and to any communication pertaining to me and made in the course of any confidential relationship recognized by law. My Agent may also disclose such information to such persons as my Agent deems appropriate.

E. *Resort to Courts.* I hereby authorize my Agent to seek on my behalf and at my expense:

(1) A declaratory judgment from any court of competent jurisdiction interpreting the validity of this document or any of the acts authorized by this document, but such declaratory judgment shall not be necessary in order for my Agent to perform any act authorized by this document; or

(2) A mandatory injunction requiring compliance with my Agent's instructions by any person obligated to comply with instructions given by my Agent; or

(3) Actual and punitive damages against any person obligated to comply with instructions given by my Agent who negligently or willfully fails or refuses to follow such instructions.

IV.

MISCELLANEOUS

A. *Revocation and Amendment.* I revoke all prior Durable Powers of Attorney for Health Care that I may have executed, and I retain the right to revoke or amend this document in writing and substitute other agents in place of the attorney-in-fact appointed herein. Revocations of or amendments to this document shall be made in writing, executed by me as provided in _____ and shall be attached to the original of this document. Copies of such amendments or revocations shall also be delivered to my Agent and any other persons to whom I have delivered a copy of this document. Notwithstanding anything herein to the contrary, I retain the right to: (1) revoke the appointment of my Agent by notifying said Agent orally or in writing, and (2) revoke the authority granted to my Agent to make health care decisions by notifying the health care provider orally or in writing.

B. *Nomination of Conservator.* In accordance with _____, I hereby nominate my Agent to serve as Conservator of my person if any court of competent jurisdiction receives and is asked to act upon a petition by any person to appoint such a Conservator for my person.

C. *Severability.* If any provision of this document is determined to be invalid or unenforceable under applicable law, such provision shall be ineffective without in any way affecting the remaining portions.

D. Reimbursement of Costs. My Agent shall be entitled to reimbursement for all reasonable costs and expenses actually incurred and paid by my Agent on my behalf under any provision of this document; however, my Agent shall not be entitled to compensation for services rendered hereunder.

E. *Conflict of Interest.* I recognize and acknowledge that my Agent may be entitled to a portion of my estate upon my death in accordance with my Last Will and Testament and that such entitlement may give rise to a conflict of interest. Nevertheless, I believe that the individual appointed as my Agent hereunder are those most concerned about my welfare and most knowledgeable about my beliefs, preferences and values with respect to medical treatment and decisions that may need to be made on my behalf in the future. Accordingly, I appoint said individuals with the knowledge of such potential conflict of interest.

F. *Resignation of Agent.* (1) My Agent may resign by executing a written resignation and delivering such resignation to me, or if I am mentally incapacitated, by delivering such to any Durable Power of Attorney for Property that I may execute and is then in effect, and to the Conservator of my person or property or both that may have been appointed by a court of competent jurisdiction, or if no such attorney-in-fact or Conservator is then serving, to any person with whom I am then residing or who then has the care and custody of me.

(2) The incapacity of my Agent shall be deemed a resignation by such individual as Agent. *For purposes of this paragraph, a person's incapacity shall be deemed to exist when the person's incapacity has been declared by a court of competent jurisdiction, or when a Conservator for such person has been appointed, or upon presentation of a certificate executed by two (2) physicians licensed to practice in the state of such person's residence that states it is the physicians' opinions that the Agent is incapable of caring for him/herself and/or is physically or mentally incapable of managing his/her personal or financial affairs.* The effective date of such incapacity shall be the date of the decree adjudicating the incapacity, the date of the decree appointing the Conservator or the date of the physicians' certificate, as the case may be.

G. *Exculpation.* My Agent, her estate, heirs, successors and assigns are hereby released and forever discharged by me, my estate, heirs, successors and assigns from all liability and from all claims or demands of all kinds arising out of the acts or omissions of my Agent, except for willful misconduct or gross negligence.

H. *Governing Law.* This power is to be construed as a Durable Power of Attorney for Health Care as defined in Section _____ of the _____ Code Annotated. This document shall be governed by the laws of the State of _____ in all respects, including its validity, construction, interpretation, and termination. I intend for this Durable Power of Attorney for Health Care to be honored in any jurisdiction where it may be presented and for any such jurisdiction to refer to _____ law to interpret and determine the validity of this document and any of the powers granted under this document. This power of attorney shall not be affected by my subsequent disability or incapacity.

I have discussed with my Agent the significance of the powers granted herein and do hereby execute this Durable Power of Attorney for Health Care on this _____ day of _____, 20xx. *In so doing, I understand that (1) this document gives my attorney-in-fact very broad powers relating to my health and well-being; (2) the powers granted herein continue after I am disabled or incapacitated; (3) I can amend or revoke this document in writing at any time; (4) I can revoke the appointment of my attorney-in-fact by notifying my Agent orally or in writing; and (5) I can revoke the authority of my attorney-in-fact to make health care decisions by notifying the health care provider orally or in writing.*

_____

STATEMENT OF WITNESSES

STATE OF _____

COUNTY OF _____

We, _____ and _____, the subscribing witnesses hereto under penalty of perjury under the laws of _____:

1. *The person who signed or acknowledged this document is personally known to us to be the principal;*

2. *The principal signed or acknowledged this Durable Power of Attorney for Health Care in our presence;*

3. *The principal appears to be of sound mind and under no duress, fraud or undue influence, fully aware of the action taken herein and its possible consequence.*

4. *We are not appointed as Agent for health care decisions by the document;*

5. *We are not related to _____ by blood, marriage or adoption;*

6. *To the best of our knowledge we are not entitled to any portion of the Estate of _____ upon his/her death under any Will or Codicil thereto presently existing or by operation of law;*

7. *We are not the attending physician or employee of such physician or health care facility in which _____ is a patient;*

8. We are not a health care provider, an employee of a health care provider, the operator of a community care facility or an employee of an operator of a community care facility;

9. *And we are not a person who, at the present time, has a claim against any portion of the Estate of _____ upon his/her death.*

_____

Witness

_____

Witness

_____

Subscribed and sworn to and acknowledged before me by _____ and _____ witnesses to said Durable Power of Attorney for Health Care, this _____ day of _____, 20xx.

_____

Notary Public

My Commission Expires: _____

DURABLE POWER OF ATTORNEY
FOR HEALTH CARE
WARNING TO PERSON EXECUTING THIS DOCUMENT

THIS IS AN important legal document. Before executing this document, you should know these important facts:

THIS DOCUMENT GIVES the person you designate as your Agent (the attorney-in-fact) the power to make health care decisions for you. Your Agent must act consistently with your desires as stated in this document.

EXCEPT AS YOU otherwise specify in this document, this document gives your Agent, among other powers, the power to consent to your doctor not giving treatment or stopping treatment necessary to keep you alive.

NOTWITHSTANDING THIS DOCUMENT, you have the right to make medical and other health care decisions for yourself so long as you can give informed consent with respect to the particular decision. In addition, no treatment may be given to you over your objection, and health care necessary to keep you alive may not be stopped or withheld if you object at the time.

THIS DOCUMENT GIVES your Agent authority to consent, to refuse to consent, or to withdraw consent to any care, treatment, service, or procedure to maintain, diagnose or treat a physical or mental condition. This power is subject to any limitations that you include in this document. You may state in this document any types of treatment that you do not desire. In addition, a court can take away the power of your Agent to make health care decisions for you if your Agent: (1) authorizes anything that is illegal, or (2) acts contrary to your desires as stated in this document.

YOU HAVE THE right to revoke the authority of your Agent by notifying your Agent or your treating physician, hospital or other health care provider orally or in writing of the revocation.

YOUR AGENT HAS the right to examine your medical records and to consent to their disclosure unless you limit this right in this document.

UNLESS YOU OTHERWISE specify in this document, this document gives your Agent the power after you die to: (1) authorize an autopsy, (2) donate your body or parts thereof for transplant or therapeutic or educational or scientific purposes, and (3) direct the disposition of your remains.

IF THERE IS anything in this document that you do not understand, you should ask a lawyer to explain it to you.

AUTHORIZATION FOR USE AND DISCLOSURE OF PROTECTED HEALTH INFORMATION

1. I, _____, authorize all health care providers, including physicians, nurses, and all other persons (including entities) who may have provided, or be providing me with any type of health care, to disclose all of my protected health information:

___(A) TO AN agent designated in a Durable Power of Attorney for Health Care signed by me when asked by my Agent to do so for the purpose of determining my capacity as defined in the power of attorney or by governing law;

___(B) TO THE Trustee, or a designated successor Trustee, of any trust of which I am a beneficiary, or a Trustee when asked to do so for the purpose of determining my capacity as defined in the trust;

___(C) TO ANY partner of any partnership or other entities of which I am a member for the purpose of determining my capacity as defined in the partnership agreement;

___(D) TO MY lawyer, _____ , for the purposes of determining my capacity to make inter vivos gifts, to execute estate planning documents, and whether, and to what extent, a guardianship or other protective proceedings for me is necessary or desirable;

___(E) TO A Conservator, if one is appointed for me, for the purpose of determining whether, and to what extent, a Conservatorship or other protective proceedings for me is necessary or desirable; and

___(F) TO _____

_____

2. THIS AUTHORIZATION is voluntary and intended to provide my health care providers with the authorization necessary to allow each of them to disclose protected health information regarding me to the persons described in paragraph (l)(a)-(f) above for the purpose of allowing each of them to make the specified determinations regarding

my capacity or need for protective proceedings.

3. I UNDERSTAND THAT ANY HEALTH CARE PROVIDER WHO RECEIVES THIS AUTHORIZATION WILL NOT CONDITION MY TREATMENT ON AN AUTHORIZATION, EXCEPT FOR AN AUTHORIZATION FOR RESEARCH-RELATED TREATMENT.

4. *I understand that none of the persons described in paragraph (l)(a)-(f) above, to whom I authorize disclosure of my personal data, are health plans, health care providers, or clearinghouses, and that information disclosed by a health care provider pursuant to this authorization is subject to redisclosure and may no longer be protected by the privacy rules of 45 CFR § 164.*

5. *This authorization may be revoked by a writing signed by me or by my personal representative, except to the extent that action has been taken in reliance on this statement.*

6. *This authorization shall expire three (3) years after my death unless validly revoked before that date.*

Signed: _____

Date: _____

STATE OF _____

COUNTY OF _____

I hereby certify that on this day before me, an officer duly authorized in the state and county aforesaid to take acknowledgments, personally appeared _____ known to me to be the person described in and who executed the foregoing instrument and acknowledged before me that he/she executed the same.

Witness my hand and official seal in the county and state last aforesaid this _____ day of _____, 20xx.

_____

Notary Public

My Commission Expires: _____

THIS IS AN EXAMPLE ONLY. Living Wills vary from case to case and state to state.

LIVING WILL

I, _____, willfully and voluntarily make known my desire that my dying shall not be artificially prolonged under the circumstances set forth below, and do hereby declare:

If at any time I should have a terminal condition and my attending physician has determined there is no reasonable medical expectation of recovery and which, as a medical probability, will result in my death, regardless of the use or discontinuance of medical treatment implemented for the purpose of sustaining life, or the life process, I direct that medical care be withheld or withdrawn, and that I be permitted to die naturally with only the administration of medications or the performance of any medical procedure deemed necessary to provide me with comfortable care or to alleviate pain.

ARTIFICIALLY PROVIDED NOURISHMENT AND FLUIDS: By checking the appropriate line below I specifically:

_____request that I be given artificially provided food, water, or other nourishment or fluids.

_____request that **I NOT** be given artificially provided food, water, or other nourishment or fluids.

ORGAN DONOR CERTIFICATION: Notwithstanding my previous declaration relative to the withholding or withdrawal of life-prolonging procedures, if as indicated below I have expressed my desire to donate my organs and/or tissues for transplantation, or any of them as specifically designated herein, I do direct my attending physician, if I have been determined dead according to _____, to maintain me on artificial support systems only for the period of time required to maintain the viability of and to remove such organs and/or tissues. *By checking the appropriate line below I specifically:*

_____ desire to donate my organs and/or tissues for transplantation.

_____ desire to donate my _____

_____ **DO NOT** desire to donate my organs or tissues for transplantation.

In the absence of my ability to give directions regarding my medical care, it is my intention that this declaration shall be honored by my family and physician as the final expression of my legal right to refuse medical care and accept the consequences of such refusal.

The definitions of terms used herein shall be as set forth in the _____ Right to Natural Death Act, _____. *I understand the full import of this declaration, and I am emotionally and mentally competent to make this declaration.* In acknowledgment whereof, I do herein after affix my signature on this the _____ day of _____, 20xx.

_____

Declarant

We, the subscribing witnesses hereto, are personally acquainted with and subscribe our names hereto at the request of the Declarant, an adult, whom we believe to be of sound mind, the action taken herein and its possible consequence.

We, the undersigned witnesses, further declare that we are not related to the Declarant by blood or marriage; that we are not entitled to any portion of the estate of the Declarant upon her death under any will or codicil thereto presently existing or by operation of law then existing; that we are not the attending physician, an employee of the attending physician or a health facility in which the Declarant is a patient; and that we are not persons who, at the present time, have a claim against any portion of the estate of the Declarant upon his/her death.

_____

Witness

_____

Witness

Subscribed, sworn to and acknowledged before me by

_____, the Declarant, and subscribed and sworn to before me by _____ and _____, witnesses, this _____ day of _____, 20xx.

_____

Notary Public

My Commission Expires: _____

THIS IS AN EXAMPLE ONLY. Last Wills and Testaments vary from case to case and state to state.

Last Will and Testament
of

_____

I, _____, RESIDENT in the City of _____, County of _____, State of _____, being of sound mind and disposing memory and not acting under duress or undue influence, and fully understanding the nature and extent of all my property and of this disposition thereof, do hereby make, publish, and declare this document to be my Last Will and Testament, and do hereby revoke any and all other wills and codicils heretofore made by me.

FIRST:

I DIRECT THAT all my debts, and expenses of my last illness, funeral, and burial, be paid as soon after my death as may be reasonably convenient, and I hereby authorize my Personal Representative (or Executor), hereinafter appointed, to settle and discharge, in his or her absolute discretion, any claims made against my estate.

I FURTHER DIRECT that my Personal Representative (or Executor) shall pay out of my estate any and all estate and inheritance taxes payable by reason of my death in respect of all items included in the computation of such taxes, whether passing under this Will or otherwise. Said taxes shall be paid by my Personal Representative (or Executor) or Trustee as if such taxes were my debts without recovery of any part of such tax payments from anyone who receives any item included in such computation.

SECOND:

THE ENTIRE RESIDUE of the property owned by me at my death real and personal and wherever situate, I devise and bequeath to my Trustees appointed under the _____ Family Inter Vivos Trust Agreement signed by myself as Grantor and dated the _____ day of _____, 20xx, to be held for the purposes and distributed as therein provided, and also in accordance with any amendments to said Trust made prior to my death. It is my intention that said Trust be administered free from the continuing control of the court having jurisdiction of the settlement of its accounts or the power of any beneficiary to bring suit for an accounting.

IF FOR ANY reason, property may not pass or does not pass by way of or through the before-mentioned, are specifically made a part of this Will by reference and all properties shall be held, administered, and distributed pursuant to the terms thereof, and the Personal Representative (or Executor) will assume and perform all of the duties of the Trustee.

THIRD:

MY PERSONAL REPRESENTATIVE (or Executor) is to act without bond and to the maximum amount possible without court supervision or control so that the estate can be settled as much as possible as a nonintervention proceeding. I nominate and appoint the following people in the following order of priority as Personal Representative (or Executor) until one such person qualifies.

MY WIFE/HUSBAND, _____

MY DAUGHTER, _____

MY SON, _____

_____, WHO CURRENTLY resides at _____

_____

_____ TRUST COMPANY, a _____ Corporation

I GRANT TO my Personal Representative (or Executor) full power to do everything in administering my estate that said Personal Representative (or Executor) deems to be for the best interest of my beneficiaries.

FOURTH:

IF THERE IS no sufficient evidence as to whether my husband/wife survived me, the provisions of my Will shall be given effect in like manner as if she had indubitably survived me and died immediately after my death.

FIFTH:

OF THE PROVISIONS made herein for the benefit of my husband/wife, an amount equal to the maximum allowable widow's (widower's) statutory interest in his/her wife's/husband's property, if any, shall be deemed received by my husband/wife by operation of law as such statutory interest, and only the excess, if any, over such amount shall be deemed received under the provisions of this Will.

SIXTH:

IF ANY BENEFICIARY under this Will, or any trust herein mentioned, contests or attacks this Will or any of its provisions, any share or interest in my estate given to that contesting beneficiary under this Will is revoked and shall be disposed of in the same manner provided herein as if that contesting beneficiary had predeceased me.

SEVENTH:

MY PERSONAL REPRESENTATIVE shall elect under Section 2056(b)(7) of the Internal Revenue Code of 1954, as amended, or other similar statute then in force, to qualify the Marital Trust or the Q-TIP Trust as established by me under Article III, of the _____ Trust Agreement dated the _____ day of _____, 20xx, for the federal estate tax marital deduction.

EIGHTH:

I HEREBY APPOINT to serve without bond as guardian over the persons and properties of my minor children the following people in the following priority:

MY HUSBAND/WIFE, _____

MY SISTER, _____

MY BROTHER, _____

NINTH:

UPON MY DEATH it is my wish that my body and essence undergo the rites of Mummification and Transference. To that end, I specifically direct the following:

THE RITES OF my Mummification and Transference will be conducted by SUMMUM, a 501(c)(3) organization. Upon my death, I donate my body to SUMMUM for the purpose of conducting my Mummification and Transference.

MY BODY SHALL be delivered as soon after my death as practicable and to the full extent legally possible, without autopsy or embalming, to a funeral home designated by SUMMUM.

THE FUNERAL HOME designated by SUMMUM and given a copy of this Last Will shall carry out specific instructions as directed by SUMMUM in order to prepare and facilitate the transportation of my body to a sanctuary that will be designated by SUMMUM when the time comes.

UPON THE COMPLETION of my Mummification and Transference, I direct that my body be enshrined/entombed at: _____.

I HAVE MADE pre-arrangements with SUMMUM for my Mummification and Transference. Because the rites of Mummification and Transference are very elaborate, detailed, thorough, and lengthy, SUMMUM incurs an extensive cost to carry out these rites. Therefore, I have arranged a donation to SUMMUM which will assist the organization in carrying out my wishes.

TENTH:

THIS WILL HAS been prepared in duplicate, each copy of which has been executed as an original. One of these executed copies is in my possession and the other is deposited for safekeeping with my attorney, _____. Either of these wills is to be considered as the original. If only one copy of this Will can be found, then it shall be considered as the original, and the missing copy will be presumed inadvertently lost. Any clarifications or instructions concerning this Will may be obtained by calling the above-mentioned attorney who is requested to do everything necessary to implement the provisions of this Will.

IN WITNESS WHEREOF, I, _____, the testator/testatrix, sign my name to this instrument consisting of ___ pages this _____ day of _____, 20xx, and being first duly sworn, do hereby declare to the undersigned authority that I sign and execute this instrument as my Last Will and that I sign it willingly (or willingly direct another to sign for me), that I execute it as my free and voluntary act for the purposes expressed in it, and that I an 18 years of age or older, of sound mind, and under no constraint or undue influence.

_____

TESTATOR/TESTATRIX

WE, _____ AND _____, the witnesses, sign our names to this instrument, being first duly sworn, and do hereby declare to the undersigned authority that the testator/testatrix declares it to be his/her Last Will and requested us to sign as witnesses thereof, and that he/she signs it willingly (or willingly directs another to sign for him/her), and that each of us, in the presence and hearing of the testator/testatrix and of each other, hereby signs this Will as witness to the testator's/testatrix's signing, and that to the best of our knowledge the testator/testatrix is 18 years of age or older, of sound mind, and under no constraint or under influence.

WITNESS:RESIDING:

_____

WITNESS:RESIDING:

_____

_____

STATE OF _____)

COUNTY OF _____)

SUBSCRIBED, SWORN TO, and acknowledged before my by _____, the testator/testatrix, and subscribed and sworn to before my by _____ and _____, witnesses, this _____ day of _____, 20xx.

_____
NOTARY PUBLIC   [NOTARY Seal]

Index

About the Authors

Cenetta J. Lee

Cenetta J. Lee is retired and lives in North Carolina. She worked in the Washington, D.C., school system, teaching reading in the Head Start Follow Through Program. Later she joined The Ferguson Library in Stamford, Connecticut, where she held several staff positions before becoming Director of Branch Libraries.

In 1989, she founded Heritage Unlimited, a multicultural book business serving the needs of the broader library constituency. In 1993, she retired from The Ferguson Library after seventeen years of service, as Director of Administrative Services.

During her professional career, Lee served on several local and national boards and, is a former member of the American Library Association, the New England Booksellers Association, and the American Booksellers Association. She is also a member of Alpha Kappa Alpha Sorority, Inc. and a member of Links, Inc. (Alumni-Status). As an educator librarian, business owner, and community-involved individual, she connects people to the knowledge and information available through print and electronic sources.

Lee received recognition for her service to the Stamford Volunteer Center, Literacy Volunteers of Stamford, and the Child Care Center of Stamford.

She earned her Bachelor of Library Science and Masters of Library Science degrees from Southern Connecticut State University. Cenetta is married and has two adult children and three granddaughters.

About the Authors

Gloria F. Carr

Gloria F. Carr, Ph.D., RN, is an Assistant Professor at The University of Memphis Loewenberg School of Nursing where she teaches Gerontological Nursing to undergraduate students and Nursing Education to graduate nursing students.

Dr. Carr obtained a Bachelor of Science degree in Nursing (BSN) from Union University, Memphis, Tennessee campus; a Master of Science degree in Nursing (MSN) from The University of Tennessee Health Science Center— Memphis campus; and a degree of Doctor of Philosophy from The University of Texas at Arlington.

Her research interests include enhancing quality of life in older adults, especially Grandmother Caregivers and improving the success of minority nursing students. Dr. Carr has published and presented topics about Grandmother Caregivers in various settings locally, nationally, and internationally.

PHRONESIS
PRESS

www.phronesispress.com

For additional information and current resources about topics covered in Stepping Up,
visit our informational website at www.eclecticcaring.com.